Freedom from Worry

Prayer of Peace for an Anxious Mind

Karen Zeigler

© 2011 by Karen Zeigler

Scriptures noted are taken from www.biblegateway.com. Word definitions noted are taken from www.dictionary.com.

This book is dedicated to...

God - Thank You for showing me how to fully use Your Word to gain peace in my life and for allowing me to spread that peace to others who are struggling with fear, anxiety, and worry. • My family, for their endless love and support. • My Life Coach, Valorie Burton, for her support and guidance. • My coaching clients, who tested these techniques in their own lives. • My Life Group at McGregor, whose members were the original test pilots for this message. • My friend Crystal, who treated me to a writing retreat at her lovely home in North Carolina. • My friends, who helped proof read this manuscript.

Karen Zeigler

Dear Mark,

It's official the 1st book is complete & as a person of influence in my life I wanted you to have one of the 1st signed copies.

As an avid reader your feedback would be invaluable to me. And as a pastor your insight on how to pursue speaking at churches outside McShugal would be a big help to.

I will connect with you soon.

God Bless,

Karen

Introduction

I have been a Christian since I was ten so 2007 was not the first time I had heard of or read Philippians 4:6-7 *Do not be anxious about anything, but in everything, by prayer and petition, with thanksgiving, present your requests to God. And the peace of God, which transcends all understanding, will guard your hearts and your minds in Christ Jesus.* I had committed this passage to memory when I took up horseback riding at 37 in 2003 because I was extremely anxious about riding. But in 2007, I wasn't just anxious about life circumstances or fearful about a new adventure. I was worried nonstop, to the point of being sick to my stomach at times. I was an investment advisor and in 2007, the market had seriously crashed. I was not new to investments. In fact, the market had crashed several times during my financial career. But this time it was different. The first difference was that the market crashed in every sector. For those who have not studied finance, this may not sound like a big deal. Yet it was a resounding warning bell to me. During previous market crashes, it wasn't unusual for one or two sectors to crash while the other sectors continued performing pretty well. When my clients had diversified portfolios across all of the sectors, they tended to weather the storm successfully. The crash in 2007, however, left every sector in the red. This phenomenon had NEVER occurred before in financial history. Even during the Great Depression there were sectors, such as media (radio), which continued to do extremely well. The 2007 crash was also different from previous ones because of my personal financial situation. My husband's income had begun to dry up a year or two prior to the crash. He was in the construction industry. It had been the real estate bubble that precipitated the market crash. Living in southwest Florida, we were on the front end of the real estate decline, so we had already felt the effects of the bubble before it burst nationwide. The third difference, and probably the most overwhelming one, was the heartfelt desire that I had been having to leave my role as a financial advisor and become a writer, speaker, and coach. I believe this desire came directly from God. In fact, I was already in the process of leaving the financial arena, but unfortunately for me, the switch was not soon enough. As you can imagine, my explanations to clients who had just lost up to fifty percent of their wealth was gut-wrenching, to say the least. The market crash was in uncharted territory that would go down in American history and I didn't have any good answers to offer my clients. I also worried that the Lord was allowing me to suffer this mess and the subsequent financial hardship because I had initially felt Him urging me to leave the financial world, but had been slow to obey. The lucrative and generous lifestyle that my family had previously enjoyed shrunk by seventy percent or more. It was during these stressed-filled months that I turned to the Bible and began to dissect

Philippians 4:6-7. I developed the journaling and prayer process that I will outline in this book. As I began to fully _**use**_ God's words within this scripture passage, I experienced the transformation of peace that surpasses understanding. Previously, I had only read about this sort of transformation; I had never truly experienced the peace. As I write this, the effects of the real estate bubble and market crash of 2007 are still reverberating throughout the country and now the world, with unemployment skyrocketing, record breaking bankruptcy filings, and foreclosures. The anxiety and worry are taking their toll on individuals, families, and businesses. This transformation of peace that I experienced, even in the face of bankruptcy, is the first reason that I am confident God will unleash His power in you as you learn to use His Word fully and break free from worry. Secondly, I have begun to use this journaling and prayer process with my clients and their testimonies of experiencing transformative peace will be shared with you throughout this book. My prayer is that you will use your newfound *Freedom from Worry* to, like me, embark on the plans God has laid upon your heart.

To accelerate your understanding and use of the prayer described in this book visit www.inspirationtochange.org and order the CD of the live *Freedom from Worry* class or sign up to participate in an upcoming 6-week *Freedom from Worry* Teleclass. Also ask about bringing a *Freedom from Worry* Workshop to your church or organization.

Chapter 1

Entering the Twilight Zone...

It was 2006 and my life had entered *The Twilight Zone*. Not the movie, but the amusement park version with the ride, *The Tower of Terror*. The first, gut-wrenching drop came when a builder that my husband had contracted with filed bankruptcy and left my husband's company holding a debt of $300,000 with no hope to recover. We caught our breath, and then realized we weren't going to die. Things were going to be okay – my husband's income was still steady, as was mine; we had six months of expenses in cash; plenty of unused credit for emergencies; and if needed, we had our retirement assets. Then the next drop began, slowly but escalating quickly. The real estate bubble burst and the income from my husband's construction company began to dry up. Hearts racing, we adjusted, checking our seat belts to make sure everyone was secure.

We caught our breaths and realized we were going to be okay – my income was still good and our other financial resources were still intact and available. We could tighten our belts (a lot!) and everything would be okay. Then – *bam!* – another gut-wrenching drop happened. This time, the unexpected occurred. The stock market crashed by more than half, affecting not only my clients but me as well. As an advisor, my income was a percentage of their assets and thus it fell by more than half. *Gasp!* Worries flooded my mind from every direction. Fear about our financial future, my clients' futures, questions about why the fundamentals of investing hadn't held true, nagging worries about whether my disobedience to God's call had landed me in this mess, and many more thoughts crossed my mind. I began to recite an old tried and true scripture that had served me well in the past. Philippians 4:6-7 was on my mind: "Do not be anxious about anything, but in everything, by prayer and petition, with thanksgiving, present your requests to God. And the peace of God, which transcends all understanding, will guard your hearts and your minds in Christ Jesus." But despite continually reciting the scripture, I could not get the worrisome thoughts to leave. I had fallen into the worry pit and I needed more than mindless recitation of scripture to free me. I had to take action in order for the words to become real. Once they came to life, the Lord could penetrate my worrisome soul.

For me and many other Christians, worry is not easy to admit. As Christians, we learn to paste on a smile and chant the words, "Everything's fine," however unintentionally. For those who love and honor the Lord, everything will be fine. But in the meantime, we are fighting against human feelings that are, in many cases, justified. Worry is a daily struggle for many people. Assuming you're human, it's likely that you've seriously suffered from worry at least once in your life and more than likely, it is recurring on some level daily. It is this daily habit of worry that has led many, including Christians, to resort to anxiety medication and even suicide. And although anxiety medication may help balance the emotions and reduce the physical signs of worry, it does nothing to stop the deluge of worrisome thoughts or the internal struggle.

Christians are blessed with resources to turn to: scripture, prayer, and fellow Christians. But in those instances where the circumstances are so heavy - like a weight that cannot be lifted or thrown aside - these resources just don't seem to be enough. It's during these times that reciting a scripture or saying a prayer seem to be as effective as using a feather to move a boulder. Even if you have memorized and successfully recited a passage like Philippians 4:6-7, it is very likely that when extreme problems arise, these methods are not effective. In fact, more worries usually come flooding in, drowning out the passage and filling your mind once again with negative thoughts. Worry can become a sickness. We often mistakenly treat the symptoms but not the cause. For others, worry may not become so serious as to overwhelm the functions of normal life, but the thoughts of fear and worry stop us from pursuing our dreams and the goals we want to achieve in life. Whether worry has you sick or just plain stuck, the abundant life you want can be more than a "someday."

The fact that you are still reading this tells me that some of this resonates with you. Perhaps you are at a similar place, doubting your very faith and the power of God's impact in your life. If you are like me, you have read or recited scripture and prayed, yet nothing seems to stop the flood of fear and worry. It has you sick, depressed, unable to focus, awake at night, and it's impacting your daily quality of life. You have a nagging feeling that you are not moving in the right direction or are unsure of how to hear the Lord's leadings. You may be asking yourself, "Why? Why can't I get past this and move on?" Or, "I have done all I know how to do - where is God?" Though reciting or reading scripture and prayer are useful, that is not how we pick up the sword of God's Word and use it to fully slay the enemy of worry. This book will show you how to **_use_** the Word of God in a way that will transform your thoughts of worry to those of peace and trust in a Mighty God. He has not left you or forsaken you. God is listening and ready to help.

I will teach you how to drain the worry that floods your

mind, filling it instead with the hope and peace that God provides. You will build and shore up a damn that stops the flood waters of worry and plugs any leaks that might break through from time to time. You will take courageous action like you have never taken before - and where you are unable to act, you will experience the hand of God, moving on your behalf in many *BIG* and small ways. There is an estimated 366 times in the Bible that God tells us, "Do not Fear": one for every day of the year and for the leap year too, which only goes to show us that He is serious. This book delves into the way God has personally revealed to me how to fully **_use_** Philippians 4:6-7 to bring a lasting *Freedom from Worry*, a peace that surpasses all understanding, and a life that experiences the power of God daily with a dose of joy that reaches the depths of your soul. Are you ready to experience these things in your life? Can you commit to learning a simple prayer and a journaling process and practice daily for fifteen to twenty minutes? If you are, let's get started, because there is so much God wants to do in your life and through your life.

Chapter 2

Power of Transformation...

The word "worry" has gotten a bad rap and rightfully so. It's no surprise that no one readily wants to admit that they are worriers - especially since Christians, by definition, are supposed to trust in God. Perhaps you've experienced moments of fear over a situation then overcome it, only to find the situation repeating itself. Maybe your worrying is more severe and a doctor has diagnosed your condition as an anxiety disorder. Regardless of what you call it - fear, worry or anxiety - they are all very similar. Below are the definitions for each:

Anxiety: Full of mental distress; worried, uneasy and apprehensive about an uncertain event or matter.

Worry: A worried condition or feeling; uneasiness or anxiety.

Fear: A distressing emotion aroused by impending danger, evil, pain, etc., whether the threat is real or imagined; the feeling or condition of being afraid.

Regardless of what you call this emotion, I believe it is part of God's design. After all, we are each "_Fearfully_ and wonderfully made." But don't get me wrong - I'm not saying God created us to be fearful, worrying, anxious wrecks. God didn't create us as fearful beings in order to wreak havoc in our lives. Instead, I believe he created us with a hole in our humanity that only He can fill. For example, picture a small toddler who is frightened by a stranger or a barking dog. The fearful toddler will run to the side of his parent, grasping the parent's leg and looking to him or her for protection and assurance. This is how God has created us, so that we run toward our heavenly Father when we are frightened or unsure. He wants us to run to Him for protection, assurance, and guidance. Our desire is to draw near to the Father who is always there for us, ready to deliver. He is the Mighty God who is Sovereign and in control. But as always, what God meant for good, Satan uses to twist and deceive us.   I don't have to go into statistics for you to believe that worry exists or read a long list of mental and physical maladies for you to understand that the consequences are real. If you are functioning in society, you have relationships, your health, a career, a financial status, and numerous other areas of your life that are fertile ground for the weeds of worry to grow. Add to that the fact that life is uncertain (Proverbs 27:1) and it's easy to see how the weeds of worry can overtake us, hiding the wonderful garden that was once your life and turning it into an unrecognizable mess. The truth is that we don't need a lesson in worry. Everyone is quite the expert when it comes to worry, fear, or anxiety – doing it and hiding it from others. What we need to discover are ways to take our minds, which have been overtaken with worry, and transform them.

Renewing our mind through God's Word is how the transformation takes place. Yet do we even understand the power of transformation and how to obtain it?

The best place to begin is with the definition of transformation and how it pertains to our lives.

Transformation: to change from one form or another; to change condition, natures, or character

Looking at many of man's inventions throughout America's history is an excellent way to demonstrate the power of transformation. Consider technological inventions such as the automobile, telephone, and computer. The first documented written message took six months to get from the east coast of the U.S. to the west coast. The invention of the telephone, however, made message delivery almost instantaneous. Once the car was invented, the delivery of a written message took a few days. It used to take six months via foot, twenty-five days by train, or ten days when delivered by pony express. Finally, the computer took the written delivery of a message to a matter of seconds with email, online chat, and text messages via phone. As unimaginable as this may sound, what if we never got to experience the telephone? Imagine that we only looked at it or read about it, but never used this powerful device ourselves. What sort of transformation would have occurred in our lives if we never used the device? Would we still be communicating with pen and paper or a cup and a string? What about the automobile - what transformation would have taken place if we never went for a ride? Would we still be traveling by horse and buggy? And the computer – would our knowledge be limited to what we could read in books at the local library? If we never used these things, we could not experience the life changing transformations that these inventions have made in our lives. Using each of these inventions causes transformation and, as a side-benefit, we receive an exponential increase in the quality of our life. The decision is ours. If we did not chose to use these tools daily as they were designed and to their maximum potential, we would not experience the immediate and lasting transformation in the ease and quality of our lives that is evident today. While these inventions are wonderful and life transforming, they are man-made. Have you considered Divine Power? How do we **_use_** God's Word for increased benefit? How do we **_use_** God's Word to transform our worrisome minds and lives? The key is found in the definition of the word "use."

Use: to employ for some purpose; put into service; apply to one's own purpose.

In reviewing the definition, it's clear that reading God's Word is not fully employing the Word or putting it to service. So how do we fully **_use_** words – specifically God's Word - to its fullest potential so that our lives are transformed?

There are four ways to fully **_use_** God's Word beyond just hearing it or reading it. We can write God's Word, speak it, memorize it, and meditate on it. You will see the reason why each of these methods is essential to fully using and applying God's Word for the purpose of transforming our minds and ultimately, our lives.

Write God's Word: 1 John 1:1-4 states, "That which was from the beginning, which we have heard, which we have seen with our eyes, which we have looked at and our hands have touched – this we proclaim concerning the

Word of life. The life appeared; we have seen it and testify to it, and we proclaim to you the eternal life, which was with the Father and has appeared to us. What we have seen and heard we also declare to you, so that you may have fellowship along with us; and indeed our fellowship is with the Father and with His son Jesus Christ. We are writing these things _so that our joy may be complete_ (Italics and underlining is my own)." In this scripture passage, John discusses what he saw, heard, and experienced: intimate fellowship with God. It was the act of writing about it that made his joy complete. As you begin to fully use Philippians 4:6-7 in the coming days and weeks, I ask you to journal (write out) everything you experience during this time. You will begin to see, hear, feel the presence of God and experience an intimate fellowship with Him. Journaling the details of your prayer will allow you to see with clarity the many aspects of your life: God's blessings and His mighty hand at work on your behalf.

Seeing the transformation of your mind and life in writing will bring you joy beyond belief.

Speak God's Word: Jeremiah 23:28-29 says, "Let the prophet who has a dream tell his dream, but let the one who has my word speak it faithfully. 'For what has straw to do with grain?' declares the LORD. 'Is not my word like fire,' declares the LORD, 'and like a hammer that breaks a rock in pieces?'"

Worry is more than a rock - it's a boulder. God's Word is the hammer that will break that rock into pieces. To speak and pray out loud Philippians 4:6-7 brings the power of His mighty hammer down to break the worry into small pieces. What once blocked your path and kept you from walking forward in faith is now nothing more than pebbles under your feet.

Testimonial

I began to realize how quickly I become frazzled (worried) and now stop myself and speak Philippians 4:6-7 out loud. It has really gotten rid of that frazzled state and allows me to stay focused, which has been a tremendous help.

~ Phyllis

Memorize God's Word: John 15:7-8 says, "If you remain in Me and My words remain in you, ask whatever you want and it will be done for you. This is to my Father's glory, that you bear much fruit, showing yourselves to be my disciples."

Testimonials

One thing I've learned in the process of listing out my prayer requests is that God rarely answers them as I think best. His answers are always better! *~ Kay*

I am not a "name it and claim it" sort of person. There are times when I have asked the Lord for specific things and I haven't gotten them. At other times, the Lord has allowed my prayers to be fulfilled. To me, that is the mystery of God. There are things that God wants me to do for myself and other things that only He can do for me. What I have discerned from my own *Freedom from Worry* journey is that God wants us to come to Him humbly and ask for help.

But even more, He wants to fulfill those requests. He desires that we bring Him glory and bear much fruit as an example and a witness to others. Memorizing Philippians 4:6-7 will keep you connected with the Lord. As long as you have Him, miraculous things will be accomplished, you will bear the fruit, and He will gain the glory.

Testimonials

I truly have felt like I've been able to break my pattern of worrying. Worry has been a bondage that the enemy used to contain me. Worry kept me from being effective and productive. I feel like being specific with the process has really given me freedom and I am really grateful for that.

~ *Christine*

Meditate on God's Word: Joshua 1:7-9 states, "Be strong and very courageous. Be careful to obey all the instructions Moses gave you. Do not deviate from them, turning either to the right or to the left. Then you will be successful in everything you do. Study this Book of Instruction continually. Meditate on it day and night so you will be sure to obey everything written in it. Only then will you prosper and succeed in all you do. This is my command—be strong and courageous! Do not be afraid or discouraged. For the LORD your God is with you wherever you go."

Are you as successful or prosperous as you'd like to be? Could it be that you haven't spent enough time mediating on God's Word to be able to discern His will for you? Can there be true success if you don't have peace of mind? In your *Freedom from Worry* journey, you will learn how to be successful at obtaining the peace of God that surpasses all understanding by meditating on His Word in Philippians 4:6-7.

Just like the technology that has transformed our quality of life and given us more freedom and benefits which exponentially increases through its use, God's Word has even greater power when we use it to its fullest potential. In the chapters ahead, you will learn how to fully utilize Philippians 4:6-7 and experience a transformation of your mind, break free from worry, and see God's blessings becoming a reality in your life. Are you ready to use His Word more fully? Are you ready to experience less worry and more blessings? If so, join me now.

Breaking News!

We interrupt this book to bring you breaking news....

The prayer and journaling process that I discovered in my personal *Freedom from Worry* journey is powerful. It has delivered me from fear, worry, and anxiety. I have applied this method with my numerous coaching clients and they too have successfully reaped the benefits. You wouldn't need to read all about electricity to know that flipping the switch turns the lights on. In the same way, I don't want you to have to wait until the end of this book before you can flip your worry switch off. I want to teach you the quick version immediately so that you may begin your journey today. The remainder of the book will be spent explaining why flipping the switch turns off your worries.

In the following outline, I teach you how to begin your own prayer and journaling process centering upon the words of Philippians 4:6-7. I will then use the remainder of the book to provide you with the details and supporting scripture for each step of the process and why it is so powerful.

Pray with me as you prepare to read the following information.

"Dear Lord, I ask you to open my heart and my mind to the process described within this book. Please allow your Words of Truth to bring me *Freedom from Worry*. I desire this and ask that you bless this process and allow me to know the true happiness that can only come from You, through Your grace. Amen."

Step 1: The writing process. Grab a journal, notebook, or open a new Word document that you can deem your *Freedom from Worry* journal and <u>write out the following, in detail</u>:

Dear God, Your Word tells me that I should not be anxious for anything. Not...

List everything that you are anxious about. No matter how silly it sounds or how big or small it may seem - make sure to list everything. Do not be embarrassed—your journal is for your eyes and God's only.

And with thanksgiving, Lord, I want to take the time to thank you for...

Now list all your blessings. Write down the people, places, and things you are thankful for. No matter how silly a thing may be, how big or small, list everything. The more things you are thankful for, the better. Also, list the attributes of God and His Word that you are thankful for.

I lay before you my needs, desires and my requests...

Review items you put down in your "worry" section and list every need you have as it relates to those worries. List everything that you desire God's help to accomplish; everything that only He can accomplish. Be sure to ask for the smallest of details and the biggest. God is capable of answering your requests beyond your wildest imagination. Make your prayer to that God. Don't leave anything out.

And the peace of God which surpasses all understanding will guard your heart and mind in Christ Jesus.

That is the completion of the journaling (writing) step.

Step 2: The speaking part. As often as time allows, pray aloud what you have recorded in your journal, from beginning to end. You can also speak aloud the prayer when time is short and there is no time for journaling.

Step 3: The meditating process. Close your prayer time with meditation. Focus upon the last part of the verse "...and the peace that surpasses all understanding will guard your heart and mind in Christ Jesus." Repeat that section several times as, with eyes closed, you imagine God's peace washing over your body, mind, and soul.

Step 4: The memorizing process. Write Philippians 4:6-7 on several 3x5 index cards and place the cards in several strategic places where you can be reminded daily of this scripture. When worry strikes and time does not allow for you to repeat the entire process - writing, speaking, meditation, and memorizing - take a few minutes to recite the verse aloud, really meditating on the "Peace of God" section.

In the beginning of the process, when the battle against worry is really strong, you may find that you repeat the process several times daily. In my own journey, I would take the journal with me and just repeat steps 2-3 when time didn't allow for writing out the entire thing. However, the writing step is very therapeutic for many reasons, which we will explore in the remainder of the book. Unless you absolutely do not have time for the journaling step, I would highly recommend always making use of this step.

Testimonial

As an administrative kind of guy, it was really helpful for me to have a step-by-step process to follow for eliminating worry and fear. I have found it really effective. ~ *Tom*

Tips for Effective Use of the

Prayer of Peace

- **Breaking strongholds** – Worry is a stronghold that Satan has upon our minds. He does not let go very easily or willingly of these areas we have allowed him into. Be prepared to repeat the process many times in the beginning of your journey and less as time progresses. In my experience, when I begin the process during a period of extreme anxiety I might repeat the process ten or more times a day over the first few weeks. When I'm pressed for time and cannot write the first step out a second time, I take my journal with me and pray the words aloud throughout the day.

- **Use it fully** – Do not neglect any of the steps of using God's Word fully to transform your mind. Be sure to <u>write the scripture</u> and <u>speak it</u> aloud in prayer,

<u>memorize</u> it, and <u>meditate</u> on the scripture verses as well.

- **Awareness** – Becoming aware of your worry triggers and symptoms can help you identify when it's appropriate to take some time alone for prayer and journaling. We will discuss these triggers in more detail in the last chapter.

- **Find a partner** – During really worrisome times, I encourage you to share your journal with a trusted friend, spouse, or even myself, as your coach. Having someone pray the prayer of peace aloud over you is extremely powerful.

- **Falling asleep** –If you can't fall asleep, but don't want to get out of bed to journal, consider meditating on the last section of the scripture ("...and the peace") or counting your blessings. Satan would rather let you sleep than have you awake and talking to God.

Chapter 3

The gift of peace...

The writing of this book parallels my first *Freedom from Worry* workshop. As we closed out the final week, my students and I took the opportunity to review all that was gained from the journaling process. Obviously, the goal is to gain God's peace, but they had obtained so much more, but also lost some things they were blessed to lose. I want to take a moment to summarize the benefits of what you will gain and lose through the *Freedom from Worry* process:

You lose:

- Paralysis - Gone is that stuck feeling, as if your life is not moving forward.

- Procrastination – You are no longer putting off those things that are within your control.

- Inaction – You are taking action and have the motivation to do so.

- Distance from God – Gone is the feeling that God is somewhere out there, but far removed and unconcerned about you or your circumstances. You have drawn closer to Him and He to you.

- That sick, sinking feeling – No longer are you feeling worse over circumstances, but instead, emotions have stabilized and the sick feeling has lifted.

- Worry – Although losing it sounds like a small thing, once you've experienced life without it, you understand what a huge accomplishment this is.

You gain:
- Peace – God's peace
- Clarity – You will see the circumstances, the way

through, and the solutions more clearly. You will also see the active hand of God in your life.

- Courage – When you see more clearly, you begin to experience the courage to move forward; courage to take steps in the right direction

- Confidence – Clarity begets courage and courage begets confidence. This increased confidence is in yourself and in God's desire and ability to act on your behalf.

- Closeness to God – As you practice this intimate conversation with God through the prayer and journaling, you will begin to experience a closeness to Him that you may not have experienced before.

- Freedom – You will experience a lightness. The burden of worry has been lifted and is a very freeing feeling.

- Deeper trust in God – Over the course of the class, participants experienced God acting on their behalf in big and small ways. It is these confirmations that God exists, that He cares, and that He provides that will increase your trust in Him.

- Influence – People are watching as you wade through life's troubles and the peace of God will stand out. The opportunities in which you can be an example and an encouragement to others will multiply tremendously.

The bottom line is this: you will have lost and gained a tremendous amount by putting the principles taught in this book to use. So let's get started!

Testimonial

I have truly felt like my chains of worry have broken away. Worry was a bondage that the enemy used to keep me in. Worry kept me from being effective and productive. I feel like being specific with the process has really given me freedom and I am really grateful for that. *~Christine*

Chapter 4

Do not be anxious for anything...

My childhood involved more pain than any child should bear in my opinion. My mother died when I was a toddler and my father deemed mentally incapacitated upon returning from the Vietnam War was unfit to raise me. The courts, in their infinite wisdom, deemed my grandparents on my Mother's side to be the best caregivers. My grandfather had been a life-long alcoholic and my grandmother bitter of the experience of raising 5 kids under those conditions was less than thrilled to be burdened to repeat the process. This wasn't even the worst of it. Needless to say, by the time I hit my twenties; I was depressed and needed counseling, despite having a great husband, wonderful job, and a good life. I remember my first session with the counselor clearly. She asked only a few questions, listening attentively as I poured out the whole horrid mess. There were many tears shed and a lot of sorrow left behind in the room that day. But it's not the ugliness of what I shared that I remember so much as the relief. I felt so free! No longer did I have to bear the pain alone. By telling my story to someone else, I purged myself of the pain, leaving it behind. In the letting go there was a completion to the forgiveness I had been trying to accomplish for many years.

The first section of your journaling (listing all that you are anxious about) is very much like that counseling session. This is your opportunity to pour out to God (the Ultimate Counselor) all the pains, fears, and doubts that are consuming you. Clean out every worrisome thought that has clogged your mind and kept you from moving forward in life. Be sure to write down everything in order to complete this "cleaning" of the mind. You will feel lighter and freer, just as I did after my counseling session. However, when you clean out the closest, there is more to it than simply removing everything. You must examine the contents: decide what's worth keeping and what needs to be discarded. Do you have items you'd like to give to someone else? Throughout the rest of this chapter, we will examine the various scriptures that support this section of the prayer. I'll provide you with additional questions to ask yourself about the list you have made, and share truths from God's Word.

Confession is good for the soul. 1 John 1:9 says, "If we confess our sins, he is faithful and just and will forgive us our sins and purify us from all unrighteousness." Purging the black gunk of worry from our minds is more than just cleaning; it is confessing. Although our foundation verse of Philippians 4:6-7 is not in the top ten of commandments, it is a command. God clearly tells us DO NOT be anxious about anything. There are no caveats or special circumstances under which we can or should worry. Journaling about everything that causes you anxiety and then praying through your list, one by one, is a true act of confession. Pouring out your burdens, letting go so that God may work within you, and focusing on your plan of action is essential.

Bringing light into the darkness. Ephesians 5:13-14 states, "But everything exposed by the light becomes visible, for it is light that makes everything visible. This is why it is said: 'Wake up, O sleeper, rise from the dead, and Christ will shine on you.'" I find it amazing that a scripture written over two thousand years ago is so applicable to my life. This is particularly applicable to the concept of worry. Since you purchased this book, it tells me that you are a worrier. You can probably identify with the fog that worry can cause. It's similar to awakening from a deep sleep and feeling as if all the cobwebs in your mind haven't been swept out yet. You can't seem to generate enough energy to function, keep your thoughts focused, or complete a task. By journaling about your worries, you will bring what Satan had hoped to keep in the dark recesses of your mind out into the light. Shining the light of truth onto these concerns often reveals what many of our fears and worries truly are – lies. I love the acronym for fear – **F**alse **E**vidence **A**ppearing **R**eal. Make a point to pray and discard all things that are false.

Testimonial

Using the writing process has shown me how quickly I go to the worse case scenario. It's really helpful to leave those things on paper and not carry them with me all day long, but instead to trust that God WILL take care of them as He promises. ~ *Phyllis*

Whatever is true. Philippians 4:8 tells us, "Finally, brothers, whatever is true, whatever is noble, whatever is right, whatever is pure, whatever is lovely, whatever is admirable—if anything is excellent or praiseworthy—think about such things."

During my time as a financial advisor, it was always refreshing and rewarding to help individuals examine their financial situation and discover whether or not they were on track with their plans. Examining your list of worries can also be rewarding because this self-examination allows you to ask questions such as, "Is _____ true for me today?" "Or is _____ true, period?" In my *Freedom from Worry* workshops, participants discuss how so much of what's on their anxious lists are "what if" concerns. In reviewing your anxious list, make a note to shift away from "What IF" to "What IS." Often times, our minds over-exaggerate concerns. When we examine these concerns carefully in the light, we find them to not be true. The world will not come to an end because of a health, financial, or relationship problem. You may experience a setback, but you can find peace, even during a difficult time. So what if you can't do certain things you previously enjoyed. Ask yourself, "What <u>can</u> I do?" Focus your thoughts upon the positive aspects. Determine the truth about the situation; this is imperative. Until you separate the truth from the lies, it is extremely difficult to determine how to specifically pray.

Testimonial

I've notice a greater sense of peace and calmness in my life. Before, when I was worried about finances or my children, there was a sense of paralysis. I worried about "What if" instead of "What can be." *~ Melanie, mother of 3*

All things are possible with God. Matthew 19:26 says, "Jesus looked at them and said, 'With man this is impossible, but with God all things are possible.'"

I believe one reason God commands us to be anxious for NOTHING is because with God NOTHING is impossible! Regardless of how long your list is, there is nothing you can write on it – including death – that He cannot overcome or help you to overcome. It doesn't mean that everything will be as we desire. However, when we leave our fears and worries in the dark recesses of our minds, they appear to be huge, insurmountable problems. The truth is that there is nothing new under the sun – others have overcome these issues and you can as well. When we expose our worries and fears to the light and hold them before a Mighty and Powerful God, they begin to appear small and conquerable.

God holds the future. Jeremiah 29:11 reveals "For I know the plans I have for you, declares the LORD, plans to prosper you and not to harm you, plans to give you hope and a future." As I write, I am deep in the throes of "middle age," as are most of my friends. Yet regardless of who I ask the question, "Is your life how you envisioned it to be?" most of the time the response I receive is, "No, it's nothing like I had planned." High school is a time of dreams. Many begin to plan for a future, such as choosing a college and major, or meeting the perfect spouse, or perhaps finding a first job. Yet most of the time, real life barely resembles our well-laid plans. Anxiety or worry about the future doesn't change anything. Even when we make diligent plans, we can not control or predict the future. My reason for writing this book is a testimony to that very fact. I was a financial planner – I could check off almost everything on the money to-do list. Cash reserves – check. Retirement savings – check. No credit card debt – check. Living within my means – check. Tithing ten percent - check. And yet I could not have predicted what happened in the stock market; it was totally out of my control. Even though I never want to go through such a trial again, the truth remains: I wouldn't be writing this book if I hadn't fallen. So if we can't get it right when we plan things out logically, what makes us think that worrying about it will somehow help us get it right.

God promises us something totally different. Use this part of the journaling process to trust in His promises and not your predictions. God is in control. He is Sovereign and He does work all things out for good for those that love Him and seek Him. Faith is trusting in Him even when the events in your life aren't going as planned.

Are you amazed at how much wisdom God can pack into six little words? "...do not be anxious for anything." God's Word is so rich and alive when we use it fully. I'm so excited to reveal more of God's wisdom as we dig into the next part of the prayer "...with Thanksgiving" in the following chapter.

Testimonial

Asking myself, "What worries do I have for <u>today</u>?" was a real eye-opener. Most my worries are about the future. But in the instance that I do have something legitimate to worry about today, I now have an effective way to let go and let God handle it. I truly am worry-free. ~ *Gail*

Chapter 5

But with thanksgiving...

As I teach the *Freedom from Worry* prayer in my workshops and to my coaching clients, they almost invariably say, "Now that I am listing out my worries, I'm finding more things I am worrying about." This reaction is similar to cleaning out the junk in our closets, only to find that there is much more there than we originally thought.

It's important to understand that worry is a stronghold that the Enemy has on our minds. The Enemy doesn't like anyone attempting to break free, so in the beginning of the process, we'll find ourselves battling over worrisome thoughts even more than before. A great analogy of this concept is found in Luke 11:24-26: "When an evil spirit comes out of a man, it goes through arid places seeking rest and does not find it. Then it says, 'I will return to the house I left.' When it arrives, it finds the house swept clean and put in order. Then it goes and takes seven other spirits more wicked than itself, and they go in and live there. And the final condition of that man is worse than the first."

But just as Christ battled Satan's temptations in the dessert with God's Word, we too can do battle. And the result is the same – after throwing the truth at the Enemy enough times, he will shrink away to fight somewhere else where he can win.

This chapter is an imperative part of the prayer and journaling process. In order to keep our minds clean, it's important that we not only empty them of the junk, but also fill it with the good things. Otherwise, the Enemy will rush back in to try and make the conditions even worse.

Creating a Thankful list is the next step in the prayer and journaling process. Being thankful, expressing gratitude for the good things, is what we must fill our minds with in order to keep worry from rushing back in. Scientific and psychological studies confirm the benefits of gratitude. These benefits include increased energy, improved mental health, and improved physical health, just to name a few. But the scriptural importance of this part is amazing and much more beneficial than any scientific study's findings. The remainder of this chapter will shed light on the importance of the words of thanksgiving and its connection to experiencing God's peace.

The Peace Offering: In the original Jewish faith, there were three peace offerings, the most important of which was a thank offering. The purpose of this particular offering was to express gratitude to God as a means of maintaining fellowship between the individual and God. This particular offering had nothing to do with the forgiveness of sins. It was strictly for showing gratitude to God for His goodness and mercies. In turn, the people would receive His peace. The Talmud explains that in the age of the Messiah (which Christians believe is our current time), the only acceptable sacrifice is that of the thank offering. Psalm 50:7-15 states, "Hear, O my people, and I will speak, O Israel, and I will testify against you: I am God, your God. I do not rebuke you for your sacrifices or your burnt offerings, which are ever before me. I have no need of a bull from your stall or of goats from your pens, for every animal of the forest is mine, and the cattle on a thousand hills. I know every bird in the mountains, and the creatures of the field are mine. If I were hungry I would not tell you, for the world is mine, and all that is in it. Do I eat the flesh of bulls or drink the blood of goats? Sacrifice thank offerings to God, fulfill your vows to the Most High, and call upon me in the day of trouble; I will deliver you, and you will honor me."

As we bring our thank offerings to God, we stand in His presence and can speak with Him about our troubles.

God's presence: Psalm 100:4 says, "Enter his gates with Thanksgiving and his courts with praise; give thanks to him and praise his name." It is this practice of praise and thanksgiving that allows us to enter the very presence of God. What use is it to present our prayer requests to God if we are not in His presence?

A 180° turn of the mind: The command of thanksgiving in Philippians 4:6-7 is an intentional instruction from God to change our mindset. A mind that is always worried is not thankful and a mind that is thankful is not worrisome. The two cannot coexist. Praying and journaling everything for which you are thankful is not the only important key in this process. Saying your praise and thanksgiving out loud throughout the day is a great way to zap worrisome thoughts as they enter your mind. In addition, this 180° turn of the mind is an intentional one: it takes our minds off ourselves, steering away from our woes and helplessness against life's troubles, and puts the focus upon God, His wonders, and His mighty help.

Testimonial

I realized early on the "Thanksgiving" step held a certain magic to it. It took my eyes off of myself and my problems and turned a fearful heart into a grateful one. It opens my eyes to all the miracles God IS doing in my life instead of focusing on the negative things. And always, after I do this step, I'm covered in peace. It calms the anxiety of the problems almost instantly. And by the time I move on the last step, my heart is in such a good place of peace, and thankfulness. I feel so much more ready to receive God's blessings with an open grateful heart. ~ DD

It's not about us: Although listing all the people, places, talents, skills, and things in your life for which you are thankful for is a good place to start, this command of thanksgiving is really not about us. What we have is limited, but what we have in God is unlimited. Our thankful list must move beyond earthly blessings to heavenly ones. The Bible is full of scripture praising God for our salvation through Christ, for His creation, His attributes, His unchanging character, His Power, and so on. Psalm 37:4 affirms the connection between praising God and having our requests answered when it says, "Delight in the Lord and He will grant you the desires of your heart."

The Bible contains more than 500 references to praise and thanksgiving, so this chapter will only scratched the surface of why a Thankful list is so vital. I encourage you to pick a different quality, attribute, or miracle of God each day and discover how it applies to your particular worry. Praise God throughout the day for it. Not only will your thanksgiving take you into God's presence so that you may present your request to Him, but it will keep you in His peace continually throughout the day.

Chapter 6

Present your requests to God...

As Christians, we learn about God's omnipresence and how He knows our every thought before we do. While that is certainly true, there is still the need to ask. I experienced an incident with my daughter back when she was in elementary school that reminds me of the importance of asking. Her school instituted a card system for lunches. It was really convenient because the card was attached, along with a school ID, to the students' lanyards so they couldn't lose it. It kept me from having to remember to give her money every morning and also alleviated my concern that she would lose the money before lunch. Additionally, parents were able to go online and add money to the existing balance on the card. When the system was first implemented, a problem arose – the parents weren't notified when the card ran out of money. Rarely did Haley, my daughter, remember to tell me. The first time it happened, I arrived at school to pick up Haley, only to find her flush, tired, and lifeless. After a few quick questions to determine if she was getting sick, I discovered that she had gone without lunch that day. When I asked her why she didn't tell me that she was out of money, I received the typical adolescent response, "I forgot." When I probed further, asking why she didn't call me before lunch so I could add money to the card or bring her lunch, she responded, "I didn't want to bother you." Ah, a mother's heart breaks knowing that her child suffered over something that could have been so easily fixed - all she had to do was ask. Imagine your heavenly Father, for whom all things are possible. His heart is breaking because His children suffer needlessly all because they fail to ask. Ephesians 3:20 says, "Now to him who is able to do immeasurably more than all we ask or imagine, according to his power that is at work within us."

This power was evident throughout the New Testament. From the miracle for the Centurion (Matthew 8:5-13) to the Ruler whose daughter was raised from the dead (Matthew 9:18-19; 23-26), these miracle recipients only had two prerequisites to having their requests answered. Those two things were:

1. To Ask
2. To Believe

You can believe all things are possible for God, but until you take the step of faith to *ask*, it is unlikely to happen. You have to ask. Maybe you feel unworthy, unsure that you are asking for the right thing, or even ashamed that you have to ask - no matter what the hesitation - it is very important that you ask.

Humility: Whenever we ask someone for help (anyone), we are setting aside our pride and acknowledging that we need help. This is a foreign concept to most Americans. We have been taught that asking for help is a sign of weakness. Clichés like "If it's meant to be, it's up to me" and other similar sayings teach us to rely upon ourselves. But Psalm 25:9 reminds us that, "He guides the humble in what is right and teaches them his way."

Recognize God's authority: If your house were on fire, would you call the local pizza shop? If your car was stolen, would you call the gym? No, that's crazy talk. You call the person or organization that has the authority to help. When we need help in life, the highest authority is the Creator himself. Psalm 34:4 says, "I prayed to the Lord, and he answered me. He freed me from all my fears."

Recognize God's power to act on your behalf: Another reason you would call the fire or police department in the above scenarios is because they have the power and the resources to act on your behalf. 1 Chronicles 29:12 says, "Wealth and honor come from you; you are the ruler of all things. In your hands are strength and power to exalt and give strength to all." God is not only the authority of our lives, but He also has the power and resources to act on our behalf.

Shows belief that He can do what He says: Mark 11:23-24 says, "I tell you the truth, if anyone says to this mountain, 'Go, throw yourself into the sea,' and does not doubt in his heart but believes that what he says will happen, it will be done for him. Therefore I tell you, whatever you ask for in prayer, believe that you have received it, and it will be yours". Are you identifying the specific mountains in your life? Are you asking and believing that God can and will move them? Are you believing that if He doesn't remove the mountain, He will provide a way over, around, or through it?

God can show his love: Just like I love my daughter and want to give her good gifts, including the simple necessities of lunch money, God loves you as His child and wants to show His love through gift giving. Matthew 7:7-11 puts it this way, "Ask and it will be given to you; seek and you will find; knock and the door will be opened to you. For everyone who asks receives; he who seeks finds; and to him who knocks, the door will be opened. Which of you, if his son asks for bread, will give him a stone? Or if he asks for a fish, will give him a snake? If you, then, though you are evil, know how to give good gifts to your children, how much more will your Father in heaven give good gifts to those who ask him!" Does this mean that we will receive everything that we ask for? No. God's work is a mystery and many things will not be understood nor answered in this life. However, we can say in agreement with 1 John 5:14-15: "This is the confidence we have in approaching God: that if we ask for anything, according to His will, He hears us. And if we know that he Hears us, we can be assured that He will provide."

Testimonial

I was so relieved that even though some of my worries stem from mistakes that I've made in the past, God still cares. He wants to hear from me and show his love through answered prayers and peace. ~ *Gail*

Chapter 7

Meditating on the peace...

This last and final piece of the prayer is similar to the last step of cleaning out the closet. It is by far the most refreshing, rewarding, and peaceful time with God. Meditating is like standing inside the closet after ridding yourself of all the things that clutter your life and feeling a calming sense of well-being as you survey the finished product. You take a mental inventory of all you have accomplished, notice how good everything looks now that it's put into the proper perspective, admire the new things you've added, and genuinely feel at peace with the results. This is the time of self-reflection. More importantly, it is a time for meditation.

In this last and important section of the prayer, we meditate on the final section of scripture found in verse 7: "And the peace of God, which transcends all understanding, will guard your heart and mind in Christ Jesus."

So exactly what is meditation?

Mediation: to focus on; review and repeat; reflect on or imagine with feeling. To engage in thought or contemplation; to consider something done or effected.

Medi-, the Latin root word for meditate, is the same root word found in medicine and it means to heal. In Hebrew, it means to growl, as in a dog gnawing on a bone. In other words, you should spend time chewing on this section of scripture. Treat this particular section of the prayer like a Thanksgiving meal that is meant to be savored and enjoyed. Don't rush through it like the drive-thru at a fast food restaurant. Spend some time here thinking about peace - what it looks like, what it feels like, and what it sounds like. Imagine God's peace as warm water running over you, washing over your entire being.

As you meditate on this last section, it is important to understand the depth of the words you are meditating upon. These are not random words - they were intentionally placed by God with power and purpose. During the remainder of this chapter, we will consider a few of the words in this section specifically.

Peace of God. The name of God referenced in verse 7 is Shalom, which means wholeness, well-being, and contentment. When you place the little, two-letter word "of" in front of God, it signifies a different kind of peace – God's peace. Not a peace because everything is good. A peace that exists despite the fact that things may not be good or perfect. It's not the kind of peace you experience when you're on vacation and you've left the stresses of work and normal life back home. It is the peace that God confirms as *different* in John 14:27 "Peace I leave with you; my peace I give to you. I do not give as the world gives. Do not let your hearts be troubled and do not be afraid." And also in John 16:33, "I have told you these things, so that in me you may have peace. In this world you will have trouble. But take heart I have overcome the world." **Transcends all understanding.** This peace of God that He gives surpasses all understanding. It is incomprehensible and unexplainable in human terms. It's one thing for people to see you at peace when all is going well in your life. But it is extremely powerful for them to see you at peace when there is a storm happening in your life. I believe this is one of the ways believers are set apart and different. This peace can't be found in a bottle or by popping a pill – no exercise or deep breathing can provide it. It's different and it surpasses all understanding. Isaiah 32:17 says, "The fruit of righteousness will be peace; the effect of righteousness will be quietness and confidence." Others may be frazzled, panicked, and uncertain. But you will have peace and confidence, trusting that all things are working for your good. Psalm 28:7 reminds us that, "The

LORD is my strength and my shield; my heart trusts in him, and he helps me. My heart leaps for joy, and with my song I praise him."

In Christ Jesus. When I first started examining this scripture, it struck me as odd that this phrase was at the end of the verse. It seemed complete to just say, "and the peace of God which surpasses all understanding will guard your heart and mind." But the truth is, the verse really is incomplete without "in Christ Jesus." Jesus Christ is the reason we can come before God. No longer do we have a need for priests or sacrifices. His death gave us direct access before God. It is our faith in Jesus that makes it possible. Romans 5:1 confirms this when it says, "Therefore having been justified by faith we have peace with God through our Lord Jesus Christ."

As you journal out this final section of the prayer, pause and meditate on the power of the words as you write them. Reflect on why each of the phrases is so powerful and as you end the sentence with a period, stop and reflect again on this final scripture, letting God's peace wash over you as you prepare to take on the day. To learn more about Jesus Christ and a relationship with the Prince of Peace, visit www.crosswalk.com and search key words "Jesus" and "salvation."

Chapter 8

Maintaining God's peace...

So how do you maintain this peace? How do you keep this anxiety-free life, this connection with God, and the ongoing evidence of His work in your life? First and foremost, don't stop using the prayer and journaling process. As we discussed, the stronghold of worry is hard to break in the very beginning and you will use the process often. However, as time goes on, you will use it less and less. However, the enemy is just waiting for the opportunity to catch you off guard. He wants to render you ineffective again, so you must be alert to the triggers in life that cause you to worry.

Worry triggers are those people, places, or circumstances that cause you stress. Here are a few examples from the *Freedom from Worry* class:

- Helping a loved one with cancer you find that upcoming doctor appointments triggers worry

- Dealing with financial stress you find that sitting down to pay the bills each month is a worry trigger

- Going through a divorce finds that events with married friends are a worry trigger

- A stressful day feeling overwhelmed by circumstances out of your control (like news, what other people say or do, etc.) can be worry triggers

In addition to being aware of our worry triggers, it is also helpful to be aware of our prior coping mechanisms. Before learning this prayer and journaling process, it is likely that you dealt with worry in an ineffective and negative way. Here are a few examples of disempowering ways that we deal with worry:

- Become a workaholic at the expense of our health or our relationships

- Eating, smoking, or drinking in excess

- Seeking escape through sleep, drugs, mindless gaming, or internet surfing

- Procrastinating on important tasks

- Allowing irritability and sleeping irregularity to become a normal part of life

Worry triggers and previous coping habits are the alarms going off, warning us that it is time to sit down and spend time with God, using the now familiar *Freedom from Worry* prayer and journaling process. Although being aware is an excellent way to stop worry, worry still has to rear its ugly head before you can totally avoid the feeling. Unfortunately, weeks can go by before we realize we have fallen prey again. And those weeks are lost, never to be regained. God's prescription for keeping worry away is found in the final passage of Paul's exhortations, "Finally, brothers and sisters, whatever is true, whatever is noble, whatever is right, whatever is pure, whatever is lovely, whatever is admirable—if anything is excellent or praiseworthy—think about such things. Whatever you have learned or received or heard from me, or seen in me—put it into practice. And the God of peace will be with you." Philippians 4:8-9

The word "finally" signifies the bottom line – if you think and meditate upon these things, God's peace will be with you. It's thought management, pure and simple. When we only let the positive in, when we chase away the negative and eliminate negative influences, only then can we experience God's peace 24/7. Certainly, thought management is no small task, which is why it's the subject of hundreds of books. I recommend a few of my favorites at the end of this book. However, thought management is a worthy goal that will change your life just as much as eliminating the worry.

It is said that life is a journey and with every journey, there are often delays. Living in southwest Florida, you can count on rain delays mid-afternoon in the late summer. I'm not talking about your usual summer rain, but those torrential downpours that cause drivers to slow down to 20 mph or pull off the road because visibility has been impaired. Ultimately, I am helpless. There is nothing to do but wait. What a great feeling it is when I start driving again, climbing back up to speed and moving toward my destination. Airplane trips are no less frustrating when I'm stuck in the plane on the tarmac. There are no sweeter words than the pilot announcing, "We are clear for takeoff."

God often stops us along our journey in life to teach an important lesson, give us a new perspective, or help us experience rest. However, it's never been His intentions to delay our journey with worry. It's just not part of the abundant life He has for us. Experiencing *Freedom from*

Worry brings clarity. It is God's "Clear for takeoff," letting you know there is a purpose in your life that He wants you to fulfill. I suspect as the shackles of worry were being broken, this purpose came to your mind more and more. His calling on your life is as unique as you are. He may be calling you to move on with your life after the death or divorce of a loved one. He may be calling you to move forward to the business or career of your dreams. He may be calling you to restore a broken relationship. There are as many next steps in life as there are people, but one thing is certain - you have a purpose. Although road trips and plane trips are often mapped out in advance, life's journey is not as precise. Often, the only step we can see is the one in front of us. But with each step forward, we can see the next.

Now that your bags are packed lightly with peace, you have been cleared for takeoff and there is but one step in front of you. Let me encourage you to step into your future!

God has great plans prepared for you.

Testimonial

The class really opened an awareness of how much I worry

and it gave me a great tool for alleviating it. Because of this

class, I've moved along in my business to where I need to

be. ~ *Betty*

Additional Testimonials

Karen Zeigler understands what it means to have worries, and she also understands the spiritual keys that unlock the door to freedom. Let her coach you through the process of eliminating your anxieties so you can move forward with confidence and purpose. - **Valorie Burton**, author of *Where Will You Go From Here? Moving Forward When Life Doesn't Go as Planned*

The class has given me a fresh perspective on worry and dealing with problems that I can't control. It has really helped me to work more on being present and in the moment. *~Kimberly*

I'm usually a really positive person, but I'm human, too. The class has helped me catch those thoughts (worry) that would try to tear me down. *~Judy*

I have a tendency to worry a lot. I studied Philippians 4:6-7 fourteen years ago in my first Bible study. I was starting to have health difficulties, including high blood pressure, so I decided to adopt this scripture as my life verse. A lot of us have prayer in our lives, but the process you have developed for journaling our worries is really good and a great way to release them to God. I am going to encourage all of my friends and church family to come and hear you speak and to take your class. ˜ *Linda A.*

The greatest thing that I've learned, and still continue to learn, is that I need to go to God first instead of worrying.
˜ *Kay*

I remember going to my mother when I was young and sharing anything I was concerned about. She was always able to make it better. This class has been a great reminder that God wants us to trust Him as a Father and to come to Him with that same, child-like trust. Practicing praying out loud whenever a concern comes up has been helpful in letting things go and moving on to what I need to be doing. ~ *Linda G.*

I shared the journaling process with one of my counseling clients who is going through a divorce and had struggled with understanding the situation. After using this process to pray specifically, God has been providing him with clarity and truth. ~ *Licensed Pastoral Counselor*

Thanks to this class, I have let go of so many worries for the future and really just focus on today. My prayers used to be pretty general, so I have peace in being more specific in my requests. ~ *Gail*

It's been really helpful to have a tool to use the minute a worrisome thought comes to mind. It allows me to stop the negative thoughts before they snowball. *~ Kay*

An anxiety that always came up for me in business was making phone calls. I would be anxious about what people were going think of me. This process has helped me gain the confidence I need to get the job done. I have made more phone calls in one week than I've made in a long time. *~ No longer frozen in MI*

This class has really opened my eyes to the many blessings I've received from God since the passing of my husband. Turning from worrying to specifically being thankful has really changed my life. *~ Linda, widow*

I recently shared the process with a friend of mine who wasn't sleeping well at night and encouraged her to practice it next time she was awakened. It was such a blessing when she called to tell me that she was able to quickly fall back to sleep after doing the process.

 ~ *Linda G.*

I really enjoyed the class. Hearing others share their struggles with worry was comforting and it was a great encouragement to hear about their successes over worry using this process. ~ *Melanie*

It was very helpful to learn that using the prayer process isn't so much about saying the right things or presenting it in the right way, but it's about having an intimate conversation with God. ~ *Betty*

Aside from becoming aware of the worry, what has been really great and helpful about this process is that I now have an alternative. This class has given me a tool to use to get my thoughts and actions headed in a positive direction. ~*Entrepreneur*

The class has really made me realize how much fear and worry gets in the way of my moving forward in my business. Even the simple things, like making phone calls, I procrastinated because of worry. This week, I was able to set those worries aside and make the phone calls I needed to make. I was really happy to see many doors of opportunity open up as a result. ~**Kim**

I have experienced a new confidence when booking of appointments. I've been able to schedule appointments with people that I haven't been able to for quite some time. It's great to be moving forward. ~*Phyllis*

I have been practicing the *Freedom from Worry* process for about three months now and I must say, I feel like I have lost forty-five pounds. I am no longer carrying around all those things that I was worried about. ~*Pastor*

It's really amazing - as I look back over my journal weekly, I see how God has favored and blessed me in the very areas I was worried about. I feel almost silly that I worried in the first place. ~*Barb*

> Email your testimonial to
> Karen@inspirationtochange.org.
> **I would love to hear from you.**

Invitation to Coaching

Just like an athletic coach, a Life Coach works beside each individual:

- Developing a game plan

- Creating daily disciplines and habits to gain strength

- Providing resources and tools to increase advancement

- Offering support during setbacks

- Encouraging and cheering

- Celebrating the many successes along the journey

- Evaluating performance and offering areas for improvement

- Helping achieve the results that the individual desires

As God has provided you clarity through this *Freedom from Worry* process, you may have discovered there is more clarity to be gained, additional courage needed to move forward, and confidence to pursue a new path. I welcome the opportunity to partner with you as you develop a plan, take each step of faith, and live the life of purpose God has for you. For more information on coaching, please visit Karen's website at www.inspirationtochange.org

Additional Resources for Thought Management

The Power of Positive Thinking by Norman Vincent Peale

Practicing the Presence of God by Brother Lawrence

The 4:8 Principle: The Secret to a Joy-Filled Life by Tommy Newberry

Self Talk, Soul Talk by Jennifer Rothschild

Thinking for a Change by John Maxwell

Learned Optimism: How to Change Your Mind and Your Life by Martin E. P. Seligman

To accelerate your understanding and use of the prayer described in this book visit www.inspirationtochange and order the CD of the live *Freedom from Worry* class or sign up to participate in an upcoming 6-week *Freedom from Worry* Online Workshop.

Attention Pastors & Ministry Leaders

To bring Karen and the *Freedom from Worry* message to your audience or counselee's consider one of the following:

- 30-40 minute *Freedom from Worry* presentation

- 2-day work shop for your members

- 2-day training workshop for pastors/counselors

- 15% discount for book orders of 100 or more

Third Eye Awakening:

*The Ultimate Guide to
Discovering New Perspectives,
Increasing Awareness,
Consciousness and Achieving
Spiritual Enlightenment Through
the Powerful Lens of the Third Eye*

- Ella Hughes-

Table of Contents

Introduction

*B*ased on the principles of Buddhist dharmic traditions, *we are spiritually capable of far more than we attempt* thanks to our incorruptible relationship with the cosmos. According to these teachings, each human is made up of *energy* which resonates at different frequencies, giving rise to various energy centers called chakras that are positioned over key locations in our system.

Developing a balance of these energies and attuning our senses and awareness to these chakras are said to help us establish a greater understanding of the deeper meanings of existence. On a personal level, well-balanced chakras can result to greater insight, improved health, and optimal well-being in all facets of life.

While each chakra has a significant importance in our overall personhood, the *third eye* chakra has often been surrounded with particular interest. Considered the gateway to the inner realms of consciousness, the third eye is a trainable chakra that can allow individuals to tap into cognitive functions that can supersede ordinary logic.

Not everyone gets the opportunity to open their third eye because the awareness of its power remains unknown to most people. But learning to take the right steps towards honing the powers of the 6th primary chakra can open the door to a new world of spiritual possibilities.

Often called 'seers', individuals with actively open third eye chakras have access to a list of skills that help make navigating life, relationships, and emotions far less problematic and taxing. An opened third eye may also improve our perception of the spiritual realm that exists within our world - a skill that many individuals who have mourned the loss of a loved one seek from the practice of third eye opening.

There's a lot to learn and a lot to gain from an open third eye, but the mere fact that majority of the population - even those that practice spiritual meditation and healing - have their third eyes shut should tell you that there's a lot more to the process of opening this chakra.

If you're wondering what lies beyond your cognition, if you want to improve your intuition and tap into reason greater than logic, and if you want to *see* the world through new perspectives, then come along as I guide you on this journey through the wonderful, peculiar, and dazzling world beyond the gateway of consciousness.

Chapter 1:
The Fundamental
Truths of the Third
Eye Chakra

*T*here are two major chakra systems that mystic healers and meditation experts tend to follow. The first is the 7 charka system, and the other, the 12 chakra system. The main distinction between these two system is the inclusion of 5 other chakras in the extended 12 chakra system which encompasses higher centers of energy in our being.

The 7 chakra system is most popular among contemporary healers as it deals with 7 of the most prominent centers of energy that manifest real, tangible, and practical benefits in our day to day lives.

These 7 chakras are located along the length of the spine and the system includes:

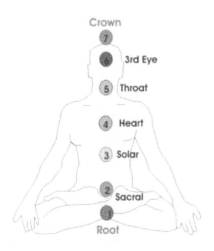

- *Root chakra* - **"Muladhara"** - The purpose of the root chakra is to ground us in our sense of self and our feeling of belonging. It supports the idea of uniqueness and helps in the formation of our identity. The root chakra grounds us in our own self.

- *Sacral chakra* - **"Svadhisthana"** - The sacral chakra is the energy center where we feel pleasure and passion from. This powerhouse encourages thoughts of creativity and joy, and stimulates abundance when properly balanced.

- *Solar plexus chakra* - **"Manipura"** -

Between the heart and the sacral chakra is the solar plexus chakra. This energy center is where your ego resides, and is responsible for your sense of self as well. The sacral chakra is a storehouse of energy whether it's positive (healing and growth) or negative (fear, pain and stress). A well-balanced solar plexus chakra manifests as assertiveness and willpower, as well as the willingness to act.

- *Heart chakra* - **"Anahata"** - The heart chakras is located in the center of your being and its purpose, as you might have already guessed, is love energy. It's the source of outward love and self-love. If your heart chakra is properly balanced, you're likely to experience warmth and compassion.

- *Throat chakra* – **"Vishuddha"** - The throat chakra is responsible for your ability to speak, to listen, and to communicate through to higher spiritual beings. The throat chakra serves the purpose of bridging the lower parts of the subtle body to the upper region.

- *Third eye chakra* – **"Anja"** – The third

eye chakra, or brow chakra located in the middle of your forehead, is the foundation of your psychic abilities. A third eye chakra that's open or active can give its owner clairvoyance, allowing people to communicate or perceive non-temporal beings in the physical realm.

- **Crown chakra** - **"Sahasrara"** – The crown chakra is the last and highest energy center in the body. It corresponds to devotion and a deep sense of the spiritual self. A well-balanced crown chakra can also connect you with higher forces and give you an insight on divine forces at work in your life and in the world around you.

  The Sanskrit name for the crown chakra means "thousand-petaled" which means that the crown chakra resonates with the most ionic intensity compared to the various other chakras in the 7 chakra system.

As you can see, each of these chakras correspond to unique spiritual functions and manifest their energy through different ways. For the purpose of this guide, I'm going to discuss the fundamental truths that surround the 6th chakra - the third eye chakra below in more detail.

Key Characteristics of the Third Eye Chakra

Also called the 'brow chakra', the third eye chakra is the 6th of the 7 chakras in the traditional 7 chakra system. In Sanskrit, the third eye chakra is termed 'Ajna', which means 'perceiving' or 'command' - a fitting name given the properties and powers of this mysterious energy center.

Located slightly above the center of the brows, this chakra serves as our link between the perceivable reality and the deeper truths and meanings that might be obscured from our worldly vision. The spinning center of energy grants access to unique capabilities that most people might not be able to fully use or understand without being attuned to the third eye chakra. These include:

- **Wisdom** - Wisdom is defined as the practical application of truth with the guidance of appropriate judgement. The third eye grants the gift of wisdom by providing individuals access to deeper truths and emotional understanding that can govern decision making with the least possible bias.

- **Intuition** - An open third eye can heighten a person's sensing of subtle realities. Inner perception is a powerful skill that can strengthen your 'gut feeling' to prevent and avoid unwanted outcomes and potential danger.

- **Self-Reflection** - Often, our judgment is clouded by personal bias. Thoughts, ideas, preferences, and loyalty to certain concepts and people can make it impossible to make decisions without some sort of personal influence on our choices. The third eye chakra allows you to explore your true ambitions and goals, and lets you destroy the tendency to execute self-serving decisions to come to a definitive solution without bias.

- **Vision** - Individuals with active third eye chakra are often called seers - people with the unique ability to prophesize future events. This is made possible by the third eye's characteristic of vision which improves a person's ability to piece together truths and come up with an accurate representation of potential outcomes of a given situation.

- **Logic** - The skill of logical reasoning isn't something that many of us can perfect because of the different cognitive factors and obstructions that exist in our minds and the world around us. But third eyes give you a clearer view of all the different parts that make up a problem, letting you formulate logical sequences that are free from the confusion and clouding that lower forms of cognitive reasoning are prone to.

An Obscured World View

What's the significance or importance of opening our third eye chakra? Why would anyone want to develop the skills associated with an active third eye? Is there anything wrong with the way we currently perceive the world?

Absolutely.

From the moment we're born, we are immersed in the world that modern society has built throughout centuries of established civilization. From the way we're raised, to the kind of homes we grow up in, to our education, our work environment, our daily interactions, and the unique culture of the society we're a part of - all of these things add up to give us a 'pair of glasses' to see the world through. In fact, even our unique experiences and relationships can add a tint to these spectacles, giving us truly unique perspectives from others around us.

This impacts our understanding of the truths around us because of the unique and specific ways our minds have been molded. For instance, compare the mentality of two different individuals who grew up in different areas of the world.

One of them is an indigenous woman who grew up close to nature. Her family grew their own produce on their own land, and sourced necessities like water from natural resources. She was taught to respect nature, and she enjoyed her young life close to a tight-knit community who lived in the same circumstances.

The other is a city-raised ivy-league graduate. This man grew up in the suburbs, and his parents worked as the top executives for leading corporations. Many of his childhood experiences revolved around the enjoyment of retail. His parents would take him to malls and shopping centers regularly, where he would sample new foods and indulge his penchant for toys and clothes.

When both of these individuals caught wind of a brand-new commercial complex to be built over a wide expanse of open land, they both had different thoughts on the subject. The woman thought it would be an abomination and a harmful entity that would destroy the nature around it. The man thought it was an improvement - a worthy addition to an otherwise useless open space.

Their differing ideas were the result of their unique 'spectacles' which they use to see the world. Each one of us might have a different idea regarding the situation in the example and the truth is that *no one is completely correct*.

Even the way you try to dissect the world view used by other people will be tainted in a way, because you have your own ideas that result from the glasses that you developed as you grew and learned.

We *all* have some sort of bias when it comes to understanding the truths around us. With that, it might be possible that we use these biases when formulating concepts and decisions. This is why people have conflicts - because we all use different perspectives to decipher the situations we experience.

Opening the third eye chakra can help us see reality for what it truly is. This chakra doesn't erase bias, but instead looks beyond it to reveal the actual essence of the experiences we have. Similarly, the third eye chakra can also help us see our own bias so that we can make better informed decisions that go away with the tendency to lean towards a specific choice because of our unique 'spectacles.'

This heightened awareness of truth makes it possible to avoid conflict. There is no one more capable of putting themselves in someone else's shoes compared to an individual with an awakened third eye. Being able to empathize more deeply with other people can help you formulate fair decisions and choices that truly put the best interest of the people involved front and center.

Beyond the Senses

From world-renowned 1500's seer Nostradamus to modern clairvoyants like John Edward, the power of the third eye has made itself known to mankind. These popular personalities are some of the most controversial people to ever exist, thanks to their unique abilities that challenge our human understanding of truth and the unknown.

One of the powers of the third eye aside from granting individuals the ability to sense truth in its purest form, is the capability to *see* what others can't. Of course, as the name suggests, the third eye gives its user a 6th sense which opens up the possibility of seeing events, probabilities, and even entities that are hidden from our human eyes.

In the case of popular individuals like Nostradamus, the third eye manifested its power through **prophecy**. According to mystic healers, the brow chakra can grant an individual the ability to foresee future events because of the increased clarity that they have in the present. While some individuals with open third eyes claim to have *visions* of the future, there are others who are simply more attuned to the *now*.

How does that work? Having a clear image of the present time without the distortion of bias can make it easier to anticipate what lies ahead. Imagine driving down a that road slopes up and down, as if you were driving over hills. The path itself is narrow, rocky, and uneven, and along its roadsides are lush vegetation and forests. Sharp curves come one after the other, preventing you from driving in a straight line. Given the conditions, it would be impossible to detect what lies ahead, so there's no way for you to predict or anticipate what you should expect.

Now, imagine flying over this road.

The first scenario of driving represents your perspective of the world by using your human senses. The second, represents how you might see the world using your third eye chakra. While it doesn't eliminate the obstructions, distractions, and elements of the road you're on, it does let you see *above* them. As you soar over the road, you can see what lies ahead and you can plan what you need to do in order to optimize your journey and minimize the struggles of moving through this treacherous road.

In the same way, the third eye doesn't remove any of our biases or previously conceived ideas. Instead, it puts everything into perspective. It lets you see where biases and tendencies fit and how they affect the decisions you make. By showing you the complete context of your truth, your third eye chakra lets you anticipate the future with accuracy.

Not all of Nostradamus' prophesies came true, but most of his predictions have happened, leading experts to believe that he couldn't actually *see* the future. His understanding of reality was simply so concise and accurate that he could measure out how the different events and circumstances around him would pan out at a future time.

Essentially, it's as though he were flying over a network of roads, able to see how the different paths beneath him would diverge over the distance they traveled. The roads were the facets that made up his current reality, and the view was his clear perception of how things actually were minus the distractions and obstructions that the individuals on land might have seen.

Another way that the third eye can improve our perception is through the ability of clairvoyance. Defined as the ability to view beyond space and time, this term literally translates to 'clear seeing.' Individuals with the ability of clairvoyance can essentially *see* beyond what we see with our sense of sight. The visions may range from simple stills to vibrant motion picturesque images that seem to occur in the same space and time as the perceivable world.

The ability of clairvoyance happens in levels. These are divided into *revelations, sensations,* and *sight.* Some people may experience it on all three levels, while others are isolated to just one or two. This all depends on how attuned an individual is to the energy of their third eye.

The first level - which is **revelation** - is similar to the type of capability demonstrated by Nostradamus. The man would awaken from slumber or from meditation with new knowledge that he didn't previously possess. Revelations are essentially truths that are given to an individual to give them a deeper grasp of knowledge in order to formulate an outcome or future event.

The second level - called **sensation** - is the actual *feeling* of an unseen stimulation. Hairs raising on the back of your neck, the feeling of being touched by an unseen force, or sudden changes in temperature in the environment around you are just some examples of the unique ways that clairvoyance can manifest by sensation.

Often, individuals who experience clairvoyance on this level can work with paranormal experts to determine the presence of entities in a specific location. However, the extent of the accuracy of the inferences they can make based on what they sense is limited. That is - it's often difficult to determine what these sensations mean because they aren't inherently positive or negative.

The third and final level of clairvoyance is **seeing**. Since the third eye is an *eye*, being perfectly attuned to its energy can enable it to function as one. The capacity to physically *see* through the third eye can mean that some individuals might actually perceive images that coincide with their present time and space. That means you may be able to see things that others don't.

This particular level of clairvoyance is one that appeals mostly to individuals who want to contact the dearly departed. But it's important to keep in mind that once this level of third eye awakening is achieved, you may not be able to select the visions you see. This means you may perceive otherworldly entities that might not always be pleasant.

Chapter 2:
The Advantages of an Awakened Third Eye

*W*hile it is true that opening the third eye may unlock new skills that give us a stronger grasp of the unperceivable world around us, there are more practical benefits to opening the eye. These advantages are believed to work by way of spiritual light cast on our minds and our psyche in order to give clarity to information and knowledge that we might not have fully appreciated in the past.

Increased and Improved Memory

The third eye allows us to experience a variety of cognitive strengths because it works with our memory and reason to give rise to new perspectives on old truths. That's why improving memory is a big part of its functionality. By casting light on our memory, the third eye lets our mind gain access to the recesses of our minds. This helps us piece together information - both new and old - by creating connections between thoughts, ideas, and memories that we might not have linked before.

An individual with an active third eye will manifest improved memory, be able to recall older thoughts and store new ones with greater ease. This makes it a practical skill for individuals in the academe or for professionals hoping to maximize the potential of their brain to optimize productivity at work.

Higher Self-Confidence and Esteem

We all suffer from issues with confidence and self-esteem. While many of us think that it's only normal to struggle with these facets of the self, mystic healers actually believe that it has more to do with *how we know ourselves*. Lacking the confidence to act, to do, to perform in front of others, and struggling to see your inherent value and worth are indicative of a discrepancy between your true value as a person and the way you know yourself.

Throughout our growing years, we're exposed to

societal pressure to conform. During times when we might not be able to fully meet these standards, we may be subjected to harsh words, bullying, and criticism. This creates an image in our minds that our worth as humans is reduced if we can't satisfy what the majority has decided to be the golden standard.

Along the way, situations of criticism give rise to obscured ideas about ourselves. For instance, a girl who frequently gets bullied about her weight will soon believe that she is less worthy of love and acceptance compared to someone who weighs closer to the standard set by the society.

But what are these societal standards?

Unfortunately, many of us live our lives trying to conform to *constructs* that have no inherent truth or justification. The things we get criticized for - weight, looks, intellect, skills, and everything else in between - can't determine a person's worth. Even virtues like kindness and discipline shouldn't have an impact on a person's inherent value.

But because humans are taught to wear 'glasses' that obscure their vision of the world, these 'societal standards' become the norm and the yardstick by which we measure our worth. Ultimately, this blurs out the truth about our inherent value, causing us to feel unworthy of love, and making us feel shy and insecure when put in front of others around us.

The truth however, is that simply *being a human* gives you incorruptible value that no physical feature, no intrinsic capability, no presence or absence of skill, and no potential can have an impact on. All of these societal standards are but a construct that the human race has developed over time to create a caste system because *individuals with narcissistic tendencies wanted to create their own truth to support the idea that they were better than the rest.*

Opening the third eye chakra helps remove these obstructions to help you see the inherent value that you have. In effect, this brand new understanding of who you are can make it easier to rebuild your self-confidence and self-esteem to make it easier to navigate the world around you without the need to battle insecurities.

Improved Capacity to Learn

The third eye casts light on truth. That's the basic mechanism by which it works, and there are numerous benefits to this simple yet profound function. Basically, shedding more light on the truth unlocks the capabilities of the brain. By being able to grasp new knowledge in its rawest, truest, purest form, we can understand the truth it tries to convey easier.

Imagine entering a dark room that you've never been in before. You see shapes of furniture and decor, but can't really pick out certain aspects of the room. The size of the space is a mystery, and you're not sure how many objects are actually in the area.

Once you flick on a light switch, however, everything changes. You see the room in its entirety, and you're able to easily memorize and understand how things fit together in this new space despite only seeing it for the first time.

The same thing happens in our minds when we open the third eye to access its effects on learning. By casting more light on new knowledge, we can easily grasp its meaning, making it easier to fully incorporate new information into our minds.

Fair Judgement

Remember how we talked about bias? Opening

the third eye chakra can significantly reduce the biased impact on decision making, allowing you to formulate choices based on truth rather than self-serving motivation. This is because the third eye casts light not only on information you receive, but on your own cognitive function and thought process.

A person who's third eye is open and active will be able to see how their own cognition plays a role and negatively impacts their thoughts and choices. For instance, someone who grew up with financial privilege might not initially see how that made his life easier growing up. He might think that his current accomplishments were all due to his hard work, when in fact his parents' financial status played a large role in the success he has achieved.

With an open third eye, this person may be able to recognize the different ways that his family's affluence affected his growing years. So, when someone from a lower socioeconomic class expresses disdain over the difficulty of adult life, our character may be able to prevent himself from saying these problems won't exist 'if we work hard' because *he knows his bias*. He knows he came from a well-off family, and he knows that this unique experience is what made his life easier in the first place.

Many experts would assert that this is by far one of the most beneficial skills that we can gain from opening the third eye. Conflicts are common and indifference has built walls around groups of people, dividing the population and sprouting arguments in their wake. Being able to see things clearly - including the unique ways that our cognition may be pattered due to our experiences - will help prevent countless arguments and unnecessary debates.

Efficient Concentration and Focus

Ever struggle to keep your mind on the same task for a prolonged period of time? Always finding yourself distracted by stimulation around you? Unfortunately, lots of different energies around us can distract us even during the moments when we really need to maintain our focus. From environmental sound, to our mobile phones, and even our own thoughts - we're never truly free from distractions.

The beauty of opening the third eye is that it allows us to cast light on the most pertinent issues at hand, drowning out other stimulation to let us see what's the most important. A third eye grants clarity and peace of mind, allowing individuals to snip away distractions and maintain awareness on a designated goal or idea.

Anxiety and Stress Relief

We all experience anxiety and stress to varying degrees. Some people may be able to cope with theirs, while others might struggle with an excess of either. Whatever the case, we all know that stress and anxiety can negatively impact our performance and productivity. Although it's true that they may be beneficial as motivation in some cases, prolonged, untreated stress and anxiety can negatively affect our mental health.

The third eye works to relieve both stress and anxiety by putting things into perspective. Remember - this eye *sees* things that the 5 human senses can't perceive, therefore it may be able to shed light on truths that might not be as readily apparent to someone with a closed brow chakra.

Worry and distress stem from *irrational thinking*. These are natural responses to stressful situations, and they often help to get us moving and acting to find a solution. But because of the obstructions caused by our obscured world view, we may sometimes over think and worry too much over things that we can actually resolve.

The third eye helps us see the truth of our situation. Of course, it may be difficult and the different things you need to deal with might seem overwhelming. But once you use your third eye to put every detail in place to show you the solution to your problem, then it becomes far less stress-inducing as you're able to formulate a sound, fool-proof plan to help you move on from where you are.

Alignment with Your Goals

The law of attraction is a spiritual theory that assumes that if a person *believes* in something, then it's likely to come true. The idea is that you attract what you hope for, and this is often accompanied by the truth of the third eye. Allowing individuals to look and see beyond the *now* helps pave the path for the future.

The third eye gives you a bird's eye view of your current situation. This allows you to map out the possibilities, leading you to the path that will most likely help you achieve your goals. Essentially, the chakra's energy can *guide* you to find the fastest route to the life you want to live, making it possible for you to align your actions in the *now* with the future you want to live *tomorrow*.

Enhanced Empathy

One of the reasons why we often find ourselves fighting and arguing with other people around us is because we see the world through our own eyes. That is, we only know our perspective, our thoughts, our emotions, and our experiences. Rarely do we truly and completely understand another person's world view, which is why there may be discrepancies in our ideas that we find reason to fight over.

Even when we try to empathize, we still use our own worldly view to try to understand what other people feel. That's why it might be a challenge to fully comprehend how others around us think. With an open third eye however, we may be able to achieve the view of an outsider looking in. This takes us out of our own tinted glasses, and helps us see the truth for what it really is.

By removing our personal bias and examining situations based on reality, we develop a clearer idea of how each person might have been affected to cause how they feel. This capacity to empathize - or to put ourselves in other people's shoes - can make it easier to establish strong relationships and minimize conflicts we have with others around us.

Improved Problem Solving Skills

When faced with a challenge, our most common solution is trial and error. We spend our time trying out different potential answers and then seeing which of these choices might produce the outcomes we desire. It's a time consuming process, and some potential solutions may cause more harm if they're unable to completely resolve an issue.

That's why the third eye chakra is an indispensable tool for individuals in positions that require sound decision making, especially in the face of urgent issues. Being able to see all the pieces of the puzzle allows an individual to use *inductive logic* to piece everything together and see the fastest, easiest, and most effective solution.

The Third Eye's Power Over the Mind

The position of the chakra - just in front of the brain - tells you the kind of power it holds over your cognition. Essentially, the third eye is the gateway to a deeper, fuller understanding of your mind's capabilities, allowing you to see new truths through new perspectives, so that you can clear away the bias that you've been forced to look through as a result of your experiences and upbringing.

Casting light on to give information new meaning, the third eye chakra is a powerful tool that can help you improve every facet of thinking - from reason, to logic, to emotional regulation, empathy, judgement, and everything in between. These enhanced skills won't only help you live your daily life with greater ease and less stress, but may also help you establish stronger relationships.

Chapter 3:
The Beginnings of Third Eye Healing

*B*efore we can open the third eye, it's important to first understand more about our chakras. These energy centers are vortices in our bodies where energies from different pathways converge and collect to be spun at a specific resonance and then cast back out into our bodies. In a lot of ways, the system of energy is a lot like our cardiovascular system.

Similarly, our chakras can also be 'blocked', causing impairment in the flow of energy. When this happens, the different chakras can manifest negative manifestations of energy blockage which may result to a variety of symptoms that include our physical, mental, and emotional health.

A blockage can be the result of two mechanisms which include:

- An **obstruction** of energy flow caused by stress, fear, anxiety, and numerous other negative emotions and experiences.

- An **impairment** of the spinning motion of the chakra, either spinning too fast or too slow.

Is Your Third Eye Blocked?

As one of the energy centers in our bodies, the third eye chakra is not exempted from experiencing a blockage. When this happens, you may notice several issues starting to manifest in your daily life. These may include:

- Clouded thoughts and reasoning, making it difficult to arrive at a conclusion
- Indecisiveness
- Often feeling confused and unable to concentrate
- Other people might describe you as arrogant or narrow-minded
- Vivid dreams that might seem scary or stressful
- Difficulty or inability to realistically anticipate the future
- Feeling stuck in a problem which seems without a potential resolve
- Rejection of ideas that surround the

spiritual and ethereal
- Difficulty putting individual thoughts and ideas into a clear, bigger picture

Similarly, a blocked third eye can also manifest physical symptoms. This is because the energies that flow through our chakras tie in closely with all facets of our being - from the spiritual, to the emotional, to the cognitive, and the physical. Some of the bodily symptoms you might experience secondary to a blocked third eye may include:

- Poor vision
- Headaches
- Hallucinations
- Sinusitis
- Seizures
- Sciatica
- Insomnia
- Hypertension
- Compromised immunity

Why Does It Matter?

If you were hoping to open your third eye, you should know that a blockage would prevent you from successfully tapping into its power.

Removing the blockage and optimizing the health and wellness of your third eye is the first step towards unlocking its power.

Methods for Chakra Healing

Most people struggle with the idea of healing a chakra because unlike a physical organ or body part, *these energy centers can't be perceived with the 5 senses.* While there are descriptions of how they look, how they move, and where they're located, there isn't an actual physical aspect to chakras. These descriptions were developed over thousands of years of meditation, allowing mystics to picture out the chakras' properties by attuning their mind, body, and soul to these energy centers.

So how exactly do you tap into something so vague and metaphysical? There are a variety of methods that you may want to consider.

Meditation

Meditation is the process of immersing your being in silence and prayer, reaching out to stronger energies around you and trying to attune your chakras to the resonance of the universe. This effective method has been in use since the earliest civilizations, and is one of the most powerful methods for cleansing the spirit and restoring the resonance of chakras.

Crystal Healing

Crystals are said to have the lowest level of entropy among any objects in the entire world. Resonating with perfect, pure energy, hovering a crystal close to the body can restore obstructed chakras to the proper resonance. There are a variety of crystals that can be used for healing, and a number of ways to use them to address chakra energy. For the third eye chakra, there are specific stones that works best to restore proper vibrations.

Pranic Healing

Pranic healing is a method of healing that has been used for centuries. This strategy involves placing hands over specific body parts and communicating positivity to the areas of the body that may be suffering from obstruction. Pranic healers need to have positive energy in order to be able to heal others around them, so it's important to make sure you've done your research to find a reliable pranic healer in order to guarantee ideal outcomes.

Yoga

For those who find calm and healing through physical movement, yoga can be an exceptional choice. Uniting the mind and body, yoga is more than just a flexibility test. This physical exercise strategy uses your body to attract positive energy around you. Combining breathing techniques with positivity mantras and movement, this technique can be a whole-body healing experience ideal for those who work best when engaging the physical self.

Lifestyle Changes

Do you make sure to observe a healthy diet? Do you exercise regularly? Are you making time for emotional and mental healing? Or are you indulging in a diet of fast food? Do you live a sedentary lifestyle? Are you always stressed and anxious?

In the same way that your chakras can manifest physical symptoms, your physical body can have a negative impact on your chakras as well. Failing to properly care for your body, your mind, and your spirit can have a profound impact on the kind of energy that you accumulate from the world around you.

Remember - *everything* resonates with energy. If you're too often allowing these negativities to enter your life, your chakras may experience blockage.

Chapter 4:
Steps to Heal Your Third Eye Chakra

*H*ealing your third eye chakra - or any chakra for that matter - is a process. It happens over a gradual succession of healing sessions, and requires your full dedication in order to be considered successful. There are lots of different ways to heal a blocked chakra, but experts often recommend using a combination of methods in order to address an obstruction or poor vibrations.

Before you get started on the actual healing process, it's important that you prepare yourself in order to get the most out of the experience. Being of sound mind, body, and spirit during the healing can help maximize the benefits and remove any barriers that might keep you from experiencing the full power of spiritual healing.

How to Maximize Your Healing

There are certain factors that act as hindrances towards optimal healing. These are often within our control. Aiming to resolve and eliminate them before we begin any healing methods should improve the outcomes of our practice.

Prepare Your Mind

If this is your first time performing spiritual healing, then you might find yourself questioning the process from start to finish.

"Am I doing this right?"
"Is this the proper execution?"
"I feel silly."
"This probably isn't working."

Stop. These negative thoughts and apprehensions can have an effect on your healing. Your mind is a powerful aspect of your being, and allowing yourself to think these thoughts can create a barrier that prevents positive energy from taking full effect. That's because thinking along these lines is in itself *negative* energy which works against any positive resonance that might be trying to move into your system.

Before you begin the healing process, try to cleanse your mind. Assure yourself of the benefits of what you're doing and adapt an *affirmation* to help you absorb the positivity that's coming your way. So instead of telling yourself that it might not be working, focus on the advantages that you've been promised. An example of an affirmation you might want to try can be, *"I surrender my negative energy and claim full healing through the powers of the universe."*

You can repeat your affirmation to yourself as you go through the healing, especially if you feel that those negative thoughts and apprehensions might be creeping back into your psyche.

Prepare Your Environment

Did you ever notice how you might feel particularly stressed in a space that's cluttered or dirty? Regardless of our unique standards when it comes to cleanliness and orderliness, certain environmental conditions can cause significant distress, making us feel out of sorts, anxious, and unhappy.

In the same way, you shouldn't attempt any sort of healing in a space that doesn't resonate with your soul. Dirty, cluttered rooms can vibrate negative energy, causing any positive resonance from being fully absorbed. That's why it's important to make sure you've fully prepared a space to help maximize your healing.

What are the factors that make up a prepared environment?

- A comfortable place to sit or to lie down, depending on the healing method you've chosen. Always seek a set-up that lets you assume straight posture as this can help improve the flow of energy.

  If you're sitting, it's always best to ditch the chair and sit on the floor instead. Lay down a clean yoga mat or a pillow and make sure you can sit up straight. For methods that require you to lie down, always opt for a slight recline at around 30-45 degrees.

- Dim lights help draw attention away from what's seen and improve your ability to zone in on your mentality. Darkness also helps soothe the body, allowing a calmer disposition that's ideal for healing. Dim down the lights just enough for you to make out the items inside a space, but not enough to be engulfed in complete darkness.

- Music can be a great way to maintain focus because complete silence - contrary to popular belief - can actually turn into a distraction and may keep your mind from fully entering the meditative state. That's because your mind needs constant external stimulation, which is why silence might make you feel uneasy or restless.

  Instead of playing traditional music though, you may want to experiment with other sounds. Calm chiming sounds are often a great choice for beginners. There are also audio files of natural sounds that you can use, such as the sounds of flowing water and wind rustling through trees.

- Involving your sense of smell can also help improve the healing process. Certain fragrances - especially those from essential oils - can positively impact the brain and trigger the release of chemicals in the brain to achieve a happier, more proactive mentality.

  Some of the best essential oils for meditation and chakra healing include frankincense, lavender, peppermint, sandalwood, and ylang-ylang. Diffuse a small amount using an essential oil diffuser and allow the scent to completely engulf your space before you begin the process.

Essentially, a prepared environment for healing is a space that engages all of your senses. Because we're all different, our preferences may have an effect on what we feel to be the best environment for chakra healing. However, by utilizing these tips, you should be able to come up with the optimal set-up so you can achieve the most with each session.

Prepare Your Body

Stimulation coming from your body can impact your healing session negatively. For instance, the urge to relieve yourself can interfere with your thoughts, distracting you from your goal. Hunger, sleepiness, and discomfort are all potential interferences that can cut your healing short.

Make sure your body is prepared for the process before you begin. Relieve yourself, take a shower, and make sure you've eaten enough food to satiate your hunger. Stay hydrated and keep a cup of water close to you to quench your thirst should it become an issue during the healing.

In terms of comfort, the way you prepare your environment will play a major role. Always make sure to try out your set-up before you engage in the process to identify any possible noxious stimuli that could distract you. It also helps to schedule your session for after you wake up in the morning or from a nap so you don't end up feeling too sleep to successfully heal your chakra.

Tools and Resources for Healing the Third Eye

Did you know that each chakra corresponds to unique objects and substances in our environment? This happens because each unique item and material resonates with a specific energy signature that may vibrate more closely to certain energy centers. Focusing on using the items, tools, and resources that resonate with your third eye can help make healing much more beneficial.

Food for the Third Eye

Achieving a balance of the third eye may require that you indulge in foods that exhibit a purple hue. Always focus on naturally colored foods, and not choices that might be purple by use of food coloring or artificial ingredients.

Here are some foods that might be able to resonate best with your third eye:

- Eggplants
- Grapes
- Blackberries or mulberries
- Purple kale
- Purple cabbage
- Onions
- Purple yams

Similarly, there are other non-purple food choices that might be beneficial for third eye healing as well. These include **natural cacao** and **foods rich in omega-3**. These foods are said to boost brain power, allowing them to tap into the third eye to achieve balance and reveal this chakra's unique powers.

Aside from incorporating these ingredients into your daily diet, you may want to indulge in a pre-healing snack that uses one or more of these ingredients. This can help fuel the third eye to make it more responsive to your healing techniques.

Crystals for the Third Eye

There are over a thousand different kinds of

crystals, and each one offers unique benefits for the mystic healer. But if you were hoping to specifically address your third eye, then you may want to consider investing in stones that are known to help address the Ajna chakra.

These include:

- Amethyst
- Angelite
- Azurite
- Fluorite
- Iolite
- Labradorite
- Moonstone

Crystals can be used for a variety of healing techniques, including *wearing, placing, swinging,* and *grids*. Using these crystals for any one of these techniques and endowing them with the right intention to address the third eye can be especially beneficial.

Other Tools to Heal the Third Eye

The third eye chakra uses the element of light. This energy center casts light on dark areas of the mind to help you see ideas, thoughts, emotions, and circumstances through new 'eyes'. By illuminating these concepts with its spiritual rays of light, your third eye gives you perspectives anew, allowing you greater intuition, empathy, and intellect.

That said, you should know that the third eye responds strongly to natural sources of light. Sunlight and moonlight are both powerful tools that you can leverage to help your third eye resonate with the right vibrations. It also helps to stargaze, allowing you to absorb the subtle energy of distant sources of powerful light around us.

Remember that the chakras are not isolated energy centers, but interconnected ganglion of vibrations. Energy passes from chakra to chakra, so a disturbance in the resonance of one chakra can have an impact on others. In the case of the third eye, any issues you may experience relative to this 6th chakra might actually be the result of an obstruction in another chakra - especially the root chakra.

Establishing a groundedness and security through your root chakra can help resolve a variety of problems that you might be experiencing elsewhere. If you find that you have an obstruction in your root chakra, address that before anything else. It might be causing the rest of the spiritual, physical, emotional, and mental disturbances you're feeling.

Finally, the third eye chakra is one of the most creative energy centers in your system. The more you stimulate creativity, the more your third eye becomes enriched with positive vibrations. Find a creative activity that resonates with your mind and soul - like painting, sculpting, or sketching. Some people enjoy writing, singing, and playing an instrument, which are all suitable channels for creative expression.

Establishing a Healing Regimen

Our chakras can become routinely blocked because we're never completely free from the effects of negative vibrations. An unhappy coworker, stressful conditions at home, school, or work, problems in our relationships, poor food choices, environmental noise, and everything in between - all of these stressors can impose negative resonance on our chakras.

So, it's important to make sure you heal your third eye regularly, even if you don't sense too significant of a blockage. Here's a sample routine you can implement in your lifestyle to address any issues with the spinning movement of your third eye:

- Incorporate third eye enriching foods into at least one meal every day.

- Create an energy grid an bestow an intention for third eye health. Keep it active for at least 1 week every month.

- Wear a third eye crystal like amethyst as an amulet daily. You can also keep a small tumbled stone in your pocket to grasp and hold if you feel the need to fight off negative energies.

- Once a month, meditate on your spiritual energy. If you sense any factors that might be hindering your third eye from being fully active, sever that energy cord.

- Try to work in at least 1 hour of creative work 2 days a week. You can mix up your technique by interchanging activities to keep your interest and creative energy up.

Chapter 5:
Opening the Third
Eye Chakra

*W*hile the healing techniques mentioned above may help activate your third eye, there are specific strategies you can use to hasten the rate at which your chakra is opened. These methods were specifically developed to focus energy on your third eye and encourage it to reveal its mystic powers to your being.

Sun and Moon Bathing

The third eye thrives on natural light. Bathing in sun and moonlight can be especially beneficial in terms of empowering your third eye chakra and opening it up to experience the full effects of its benefits.

The best time to bathe under the sunlight would be when there are very few clouds in the sky. Clouds may represent clouding of your intuition, so it's best to avoid basking in light that's filtered by clouds. A clear blue sky over quiet, natural landscapes with few trees and obstructions would be idea for your third eye since its main power is clarity.

Lay a blanket under the sky and lay down. Meditate for a while to focus your energy on your third eye. As you adjust the tempo of your breathing, enter a mindful state. Allow stimulation to enter your mind, examine each one, and let thoughts go without dwelling on them too deeply. Do this once every week or whenever the opportunity presents itself.

Moon bathing is another similar technique. The best time to bathe under moonlight would be during a full moon with a relatively cloudless sky. Similarly, you can meditate to help focus your attention and energy on your third eye chakra. But instead of focusing on sounds and other stimulation, try to absorb the energy of the stars.

In a state of mindfulness, focus on each star you see one at a time. Observe their light and imagine a ray coming from the star and empowering your third eye. Do this whenever the opportunity presents itself.

Honing Your Intuition

It might seem a little contradictory to practice your intuition - a skill that's supposedly inherent. But there are things you can do to heighten its power and tap into the energy of your third eye.

Trance Dance

The trance dance is a popular technique used by traditional shamans to shake off the attachments we have with the perceivable world and improve our connection with the spiritual realm that our third eyes lead to. This allows us to let go of the barriers in our minds and bodies that may be preventing us from fully trusting our intuition.

Here are the steps to achieving an optimal trance dance:

- Sit down in the lotus position used for meditation. Close your eyes and focus on your breathing. Relax your body and your senses.

- As you enter a state of mindfulness, take a blindfold and obstruct your vision. Rise to your feet and gently shake your arms and legs to loosen them up and awaken your archetypal energy.

- Starting from the core, release physical energy to shake away the cords and barriers that hold you down to the physical world. Imagine slow, sinuous movements that start from your torso and work towards your hands and feet.

- Release these energies by flicking your wrists and ankles to allow them to exit your system.

- Keep going until you feel yourself free, light, and released from the influence of the perceivable world.

The trance dance can be a great introduction to a meditation practice, crystal healing, or pranic healing. But you can use the technique whenever you feel too connected to the worldly reality around you so you don't lose touch with your intuition.

Guided Visualization

This technique allows you to exercise your

creativity and your intuition as a combined power. This technique practices your ability to foresee certain events using a guided auditory experience. There are lots of mystic healers that publish their guided visualization routines online, and using these to help you establish the practice can be a suitable start.

It's always best to use other people's material when using the guided visualization technique because it retains the essence of the practice. If you were to write up your own guided visualization practice, then you would already be aware of where the routine would take your mind, watering down the effects on your intuition.

Spiritual Massage

Your third eye corresponds to your pineal gland. While it's impossible to address it with physical touch, you can stimulate it with externally produced vibrations using your hands. In a dark room, enter the state of mindfulness and focus on your breathing. With essential oils like lavender and frankincense, massage the center of your forehead, where your eyebrows meet.

Move in rhythmic circular motions, and repeat an affirmation or mantra to help focus your energy.

Do this every evening or as an opportunity presents itself. The stimulation should help activate your third eye and gradually improve your capability to tap into its powers.

Yoga

Your body, mind, and soul are interconnected through the energy that flows through you. Imagine each of these aspects of your being as a sheet, stitched together through your chakra energy system. By moving your body, you can improve your intuition as you release physical bondages that may exist between you and the world.

There are specific yoga positions that target the third eye. Engaging your body in the practice of your intuition can clear away any static that might be fuzzying up your 6th sense, creating a close connection of trust between you and your capacity to perceive the unperceivable.

Here's a simple yoga routine to improve your intuition:

- Warm up with 1-3 sets of Surya Namaskar A, followed by 1-3 sets of Surya Namaskar B.

- From the downward dog, assume the humble warrior pose.

- Then move into the wide-legged forward bend with your hands clasped together.

- Unclasp your hands and assume the wide-legged forward bend with big toe grab.

- Raise your upper body and move into the warrior I pose with your arms in the cow face position

- To finish off, move into the dolphin pigeon pose and focus on your breathing for a few minutes before ending your session.

Encouraging Your Third Eye in Real Life Situations

Another way to activate your third eye would be to mindfully encourage it to manifest its powers in real life situations. This often involves becoming self-aware, forcing your mind to cast light on truth when it seems that your cognition is clouded or fuzzy.

In instances when there might be arguments around you, always ask yourself these questions:

- **Will the outcomes of this debate make a relevant, practical outcome later on? Or are we arguing simply to prove who's right or wrong?** If it seems that a debate won't have a relevant result that can be used in practical life and the parties are simply engaged in argument to fault the other, it might not be important to proceed. You'll end up wasting valuable positive energy trying to resolve a matter that doesn't even need attention.

- **Are there unique experiences in my life that might make my opinion different from theirs?** If you're debating with someone who might have had completely different experiences than you (which applies to *everyone*), then you should be aware that your differences will make it hard to see things the same way.

  Acknowledge their uniqueness and try to imagine your mentality if you had experienced the same things - would your opinion change? Use this to temper your expectations and to grasp that the frustration you feel might be the result of the inevitable differences you have.

- ***Have you been in a similar situation before? How can you expect this argument to end?*** There are certain people in our lives that we have to deal and communicate with frequently. If you've found yourself in a similar debate in the past, then you might be able to perceive what you can anticipate once it's over.

Will they be upset? Will you ignore each other for a while? Will it cause a rift in your relationship? What can you do to prevent these negative outcomes from happening without sacrificing either of your freedom to speak and express yourselves?

Signs of an Opening Third Eye

Remember that the process of activating the powers of your third eye is a delicate process, so you might not experience its abilities all at once. Instead, you might sense your third eye opening gradually over time, allowing you to tap into its power more and more as you continue to practice its abilities.

If you're wondering whether you've successfully started the process of activating your third eye, these signs should tell you whether or not you've done it right.

Dull Pressure Between Your Eyebrows

Opening your third eye involves focusing most of your spiritual energy to fuel the chakra and remove powerful barriers that might have been placed there through years of being immersed in our worldly lives. The result is an influx of positive energy that strengthens the third eye's resonance. On a physical level, you might be able to feel this happening if you attune yourself to its vibrations.

Some people report feeling a dull pressure between the eyebrows. This may grow stronger and stronger over time, and then suddenly disappear to give rise to a feeling of lightness and clarity. In some cases, the sensation might have a warmth to it, which spreads throughout the body as the third eye continues to open up.

Improved Intuition

One of the easiest ways to determine whether

your third eye is being activated is by the strength and accuracy of your intuition. Some people who claim not having such a strong connection with their ability to perceive the unknown or future events will often notice how they can now easily predict how situations will turn out.

You might notice your *gut feeling* being more active. This may come in the form of a sudden urge to take a different route to work, or the urge to break routine and do something different from what you usually do. That's your third eye using your intuition to warn you or steer you away from danger that your senses might not fully perceive.

Vivid, Symbolic Dreams

Mystic healers claim that our dreams are our visualizations of the realities that we can't perceive with our basic senses. Our 6th sense may be able to see these truths, but if we're not connected with our third eye, then it can't communicate what it sees.

More often than not, people won't have dreams when they sleep. Of course, there are the occasional dreams, however it's far more common to simply fall asleep and then wake up without a recollection of these visions. In some cases, we might have dreams and then forget them completely when we wake up despite knowing that we had seen something in our sleep. This is indicative of a poor connection with your third eye.

Once you start to practice activating its powers though, you may start to notice the frequency of vivid dreams. You may be able to recall them in full detail and even dream about future events. These dreams can be instrumental in helping you improve your creativity, anticipate the future, and prevent any untoward incidents that might cause you harm or danger.

Of course, there is a fine line between *normal* dream activity and *overstimulation*. If your third eye chakra is spinning too violently, you might have nightmares or overwhelming dreams that cause distress. As a general rule, your dreams shouldn't frighten you or cause any sort of negative emotions. If they do, you might have an overactive third eye chakra that needs to be healed.

Less Prone to Emotional Distress

Ever been through a situation that caused you emotional distress? Pressure at work, overwhelming loads of responsibilities, arguments with relatives, friends, and other key individuals in your life - these are just some of the things that might make you feel emotional and anxious.

Emotional distress is a normal response to these circumstances, but while stress and anxiety do play a role in motivation, being overly emotional when these things happen can be indicative of a lack of *trust* in your intuition.

An active third eye will give an individual greater clarity and presence of mind. That's why mystics tend to not react too noticeably - or at all - even in the face of distress, turmoil, and problems that would otherwise overwhelm most other people.

If you notice that you've started to become far less affected with certain events around you, then that might mean you've tapped into the energy of your third eye. For instance, individuals who might feel over emotional when pressured with work are likely to take responsibilities in stride once their third eye is awakened. This is because they're able to see things with *new perspectives*.

The third eye knows that problems are transient and solutions are endless. Our challenges come to pass - but our resilience remains the same.

Ease of Socialization

There's always that one person that just manages to get on our nerves - whether it be a schoolmate, a coworker, a friend, a family member, or even a romantic partner. The barriers in our mind that tend to center on the self will make it easy to be upset with people around you.

"I don't like this person. I could do better. I can't understand them." All of these egocentric ideas prevent us from seeing things the way that other people do, making it easy for us to feel annoyed or angry when they don't agree with us or when they do things that we wouldn't.

With an active third eye though, you'll find it much easier to socialize. You might begin to notice being more open to other people's methods and ideas, allowing you to collaborate more effortlessly. Perhaps when you encounter a potential debate and you're served a perspective that differs from your own, you see it as a new way to see things instead of it being inherently wrong.

Your third eye gives you renewed vision of the world around you, opening your mind to the reality of multiple truths instead of just the ego-centric truth that you might have gotten used to after years of growing and evolving in a world that teaches you that *your* ideas and opinions are the only important and relevant ones.

Lack of Interest in Worldly Activities

An opened third eye gives you perspective on truth and reality, allowing you to weigh the things you do in order to determine how beneficial they actually are for your being. That's why people with an active third eye might not be as interested in the typical things that others enjoy.

If you notice that you're starting to lose interest in TV shows, traditional entertainment, the internet, and social media, then that means you must be establishing a stronger sense of what truly matters for your soul. But that doesn't mean that the third eye will make you lose interest in things you *enjoy*.

Instead, it shifts your mentality to make you feel more interested in things that will enrich your spirit. You might notice that you're more inclined to indulge in activities that bring you closer to nature - hiking, traveling, trekking, swimming, and all the other activities that might enrich your soul by exposing it to the positive energies found in nature.

Similarly, you might also find yourself rejecting certain foods, becoming more aversive to junk food and fast food, and developing an appreciation for carefully prepared homecooked meals. Some individuals report feeling more enriched by spending time with their family and friends, saying the experience is far more freeing and enjoyable compared to how it used to be.

Ease in Public Speaking Situations

Many of the activities associated with certain chakras tend to overlap. For instance, public speaking is often associated with the throat chakra, but the third eye chakra can help improve our performance in this particular skill.

Much of the fear and the anxiety we experience when faced with a public speaking engagement comes from the lack of *trust* that we have in our intuition. *"What will they think of me? What if I don't make sense? They might laugh at me and I don't know if I can deal with that kind of embarrassment."* Again, our exposure to criticism can impose very heavy influence on how we think other people might perceive us.

With the influence of your third eye however, it's possible to relieve yourself of this fear. The third eye brings clarity, allowing you to fully grasp your capabilities and trust that you're skilled enough to command a crowd. On top of that, the third eye also helps you see things from the perspective of your audience.

Understanding how they *truly* regard you as you put yourself in a position to *speak* will wash away your apprehensions and make it easier for you to grasp that criticism is only rooted in their own, limited, individual concept of reality which might not be an accurate representation of truth.

Chapter 6:
Can Your Third Eye
Close Again?

*I*t takes a lot of hard work, dedication, and patience to be able to open and activate your third eye. And once it's opened, you'll need to make sure you focus your energy *daily* to maintain it in this state. Just like a muscle - the third eye will weaken over time if you don't use it regularly.

That said, it is possible that your third eye might close if you don't leverage its powers. In some cases, this can be absolutely unintentional. Some people who exert their effort trying to open their third eye might find its powers dwindling if they're unable to maintain the practice. The manifestations are the opposite of what an opened third eye might bring - lack of intuition, clouded thought, and susceptibility to emotional distress.

In some cases however, there are individuals who actually seek to close the third eye. Why? Individuals who *overstimulate* the third eye may actually access worlds beyond what we normally perceive. Being able to *see* visions of otherworldly beings represented in our realm can be tiring and taxing - just as a clairvoyant.

Seeing more than others isn't always a gift, especially if you've focused too much energy and attention on trying to activate the powers of your third eye. Remember, there are numerous realities around us, and as humans, we are designed and programmed to dwell in our own. While tapping into other realms might be beneficial to our spirit, there are also negative energies and entities in other worlds that might harm our being.

In the event that you might feel overwhelmed by the powers of your third eye, it's possible that you might want to seal it or reduce its power. Here are some steps you can take to try to balance out the resonance and restore the energy to a level that you can more easily manage:

Ground Yourself

Again, the root chakra plays a vital role in the powers of the third eye chakra. If you're not grounded, you may be prone to exposure to negative stimulation in other realms because of your lack of connection to our physical world. Thus, one of the ways to temper the power of your Ajna chakra would be to ground yourself.

Find a clear, open plot of land with lots of fresh air. Stand under a cloudless sky and look into the distance. This works best if you're performing the technique just as the sun is about to set. As you gaze into the horizon, imagine everything you see being absorbed into your third eye.

Then, take the energy you feel and push it down to the ground through your feet. Repeat this process up to 3 times per session, and practice the strategy at least twice a week. This should connect your third eye chakra to your root chakra and prevent you from drifting too far into realms that might cause you distress.

Revisit Your 5 Senses

Another way to temper the power of the third eye would be to revisit the 5 basic senses of your body. All too often, individuals who try to open their third eye end up using it for *everything* - from locating their friends in a crowd, to choosing meals, to deciding where to go for a family outing.

While it might be helpful in preventing dangers,

you need to understand that the power of the third eye isn't necessary for every little thing - especially if your bodily senses are sufficient and capable.

Instead of relying on your third eye for every decision you make, try to revisit your senses. Use your physical body to connect with the world around you and make a choice based on what you physically perceive. Avoid tapping into your third eye when it isn't necessary. This should help tone down its energy and train it into a state of *necessity* instead of being an *essential* part of your decision making process.

Use Crystals

Crystals can help normalize energy because they resonate with optimal vibrations that are closest to nature. Using the right crystals for healing your third eye can normalize the spinning of the chakra and prevent any symptoms of overactivity from emerging.

Some stones you might want to use include *celestite, black tourmaline, blue lace agate,* and *lepidolite.* Make a crystal grid and bestow your intention to create a shield between your world and the other realms around you. Carry one of these stones in your pocket to hold when you feel your third eye becoming overactive. Wear one over your heart to create a sense of calm and deflect entities from entering your perception.

Conclusion

Your chakras are powerful energy centers that connect your entire being to the worlds around you. Understanding how their power works and caring for your mind, body, and soul in a way that puts your energy as a primary priority can help you harness their capabilities to improve the way you navigate the world and the realms beyond what we perceive.

As the gateway leading to the realities beyond our perceivable world, the third eye is one of the most potent and accessible energy centers we can use to increase and improve the powers of the mind. This ganglion of energy heightens our brain's capacity and establishes a stronger link between what we can *sense* and how we understand the truths and realities that we perceive.

Opening the third eye chakra is no simple task, and it will take a significant amount of effort and time from your end. But as you start to tap into its powers, you will discover new perspectives and abilities that can eliminate much of the stress, anxiety, worry, and fear that we tend to deal with in our day to day lives.

I hope this comprehensive guide has helped you understand what you third eye chakra can do for you and how you can reap its unique abilities. Always remember to *heal* your chakras and cleanse your spirit to minimize the risk of an overstimulated third eye and maximize the benefits of using the helpful capabilities that the Ajna chakra can give you access to.

We are often contained in our physical world, unable to see beyond the 5 senses, trapped in the reality of our ego and the self-centered mentality that we're bred to adapt. But by accepting our interconnectedness with nature, the world, the universe, and others around us, we can become far more effective leaders of our system, achieving optimal spiritual growth to achieve a purposeful existence. And it all starts with your third eye.

Namaste.

Ps. If you enjoyed this book, please leave a review!

Other books you might enjoy

Made in United States
North Haven, CT
09 April 2023

35242168R00046